General editor
Peter
Herriot

New
Essential
Psychology

Social
Interaction
and its
Management

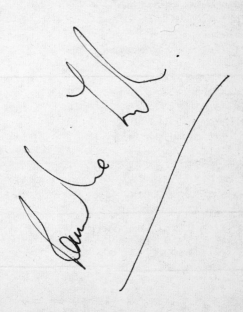

Judy Gahagan

Social Interaction and its Management

Methuen

London and New York

First published in 1984 by
Methuen & Co. Ltd
11 New Fetter Lane, London EC4P 4EE

Published in the USA by
Methuen & Co.
in association with Methuen, Inc.
733 Third Avenue, New York, NY 10017

Typeset by Rowland Phototypesetting Ltd
Printed in Great Britain by
Richard Clay (The Chaucer Press) Ltd
Bungay, Suffolk

British Library
Cataloguing in Publication Data

Gahagan, Judy
Social interaction and its management.—
(New essential psychology)
1. Social interaction
I. Title   II. Series
302   HM291
ISBN 0-416-33780-5

Library of Congress
Cataloging in Publication Data

Gahagan, Judy
Social interaction and its management.
(New essential psychology)
Bibliography: p.
Includes index.
1. Social psychology. 2. Social interaction.
I. Title.   II. Series.
HM251.G2 1984   302   83-15129
ISBN 0-416-33780-5 (pbk.)

Contents

1

Social psychologists – lay people and practitioners

This book is about social interaction and social relationships. Its purpose is to present psychological ideas about the processes involved in social behaviour, and the ways in which these ideas can be applied by those who would like to exert more control over their own encounters and relationships with others in order to improve them.

It has to be admitted from the outset that in this project our aims have to be modest because, often, the professional psychologist is only a short distance ahead of the sophisticated lay person in understanding human affairs. Indeed, maybe the professional is not ahead at all, but simply on a different route to understanding. The guiding themes will be those which currently permeate much of contemporary social and clinical psychology: first the continuity between the lay person's understanding of psychological processes and understanding of self, and the relevance of this understanding for that person's actions; and secondly the shift in focus, in clinical practice, from the professional as expert and controller of therapeutic processes towards self-management by the client.

It has at times been observed that had the physical sciences not been developed to their contemporary level the world would be a very different place, one in which we would have little control over communications, disease, food production, and so forth. If, however, psychology as a scientific activity had not emerged, less difference between the contemporary world and the past would be detectable. This is not a criticism of psychology; it simply draws attention to a fundamental point. That point is that human beings have the capacity to reflect on their own behaviour and to reflect on its causes; the human being is essentially a psychologist and always has been. And the infant science of psychology (it is only about a hundred years old) has as yet had little effect on the existing heritage of lay people's psychology. It must be clear that our capacity to manipulate the physical world is very great in the developed parts of the globe, but our capacity to resolve human conflicts and to persuade people to use their intelligence creatively, instead of destructively, appears to have made little headway. In the latter respect we may often not be superior to societies which, technologically speaking, are thousands of years behind us.

The statement about the different effects of the physical sciences and psychology draws attention to another point too. It draws attention to the fact that amongst scientists students of human behaviour have a unique relationship with their subject matter. Botanists studying plants and zoologists studying animals do so on the basis that plants and animals can be objectified, that is, as entities, they are different and separate from the scientists who study them. But psychologists know (though often in the past they have tried to pretend otherwise) that in essential respects they are the same as those whom they study. Furthermore, they are obliged to participate in the very processes they are attempting to objectify. For to study their subjects they have to interact with them, and whatever they 'find' will be a product of their own activities and processes as well as those of their subjects. In their studies they play a dual role: on the one hand they are scientists looking at human behaviour through the lens of some scientific psychological theory; on the other hand, implicit though it may be, they are human beings, lay psychologists, with their own intuitions about what would be a plausible theory and what the behaviour of their subjects really means. It is often hard to be certain what

2

portion of psychological research is based on 'science' and what portion on 'lay intuition'.

But there are differences between ordinary people as psychologists and the professionals, indeed there would be little point in writing this book if it were otherwise. In the first place ordinary people use their psychological theories as a guide for immediate action. For example a man may 'read' in the wild appearance of the boy next door a proclivity to wild behaviour, and keep out of his way. He perhaps attributes the failure of the woman across the road to get a well-paid, responsible job to her lack of initiative rather than to the intense competition for such jobs. Consequently he only half listens when she talks about her ambitions. His theories, of which he is probably only dimly aware, guide his daily behaviour, and make the behaviour of others appear more intelligible and predictable than it would otherwise. We have to make sense of other people's behaviour in order to act at all ourselves. But we are not concerned with uncovering universal laws of human behaviour, nor immediately with whether our theories are valid or not (unless we are Prousts or Shakespeares). Our counterparts, on the other hand, the professional psychologists, are primarily concerned with the establishment of knowledge about psychological processes, and only secondarily concerned with the uses to which this knowledge will be put. The knowledge of ordinary people remains at the level of the hunch. The data they use to support their theories about other people's behaviour are gathered fragmentarily and haphazardly, and are often ignored if they do not confirm their beliefs. The professionals, however, try to collect data according to the criteria embodied in scientific method, to articulate clearly the theory which formed the basis for collecting the data, and to make both theory and data public. At any point they can be challenged by others and by new data. Ordinary people can simply ignore facts which are hard to accommodate and may never be challenged or challenge themselves.

Of course we have to remember that ordinary people are many different kinds of people who vary in the degree of sophistication and logical consistency of their thinking. On this continuum we have lay people like Shakespeare – a brilliant student of human affairs – and, at the other end of the continuum, the most unreflective person we have ever met. Both ordinary people and

Shakespeare may be on a separate route to psychological knowledge from that used by psychologists as scientists.

The relationship between the thinking of ordinary people and the body of knowledge called psychology is a reciprocal one. Just as psychologists as scientists construct theories, at least implicitly, from their understandings as ordinary people, so the latter cannot remain uninfluenced by psychological theory and research, popularized as they are. For example it is a rare person who has never heard of or been subtly influenced by ideas in psychoanalytic theory: ideas about the importance of early childhood for later adjustment, ideas about the role of sexuality in human affairs, ideas about the value of expressing one's emotions freely. Many of these ideas have seeped into the collective consciousness and guide our dealings with others.

The tacit acknowledgement of this reciprocity has perhaps played some role in bringing about changes in the relationships between ordinary people as clients and professional psychologists, not as academics and researchers now, but as practitioners, as therapists and clinicians. This is our second theme.

We psychologists were not always so humble. Confronted with clients who wanted some aspect of their behaviour or experience changed (or confronted by those nearests and dearests of a client who wanted the latter's behaviour changed), clinicians and therapists adopted a position resembling that of the medical doctor, that is, an expert whose expertise is clearly of a different order from that of the patient. From the perspective of whatever theory they had been trained in, professionals would decide what the problem was, possibly employ a battery of tests to probe the diagnosis further, and set in motion some regime of retraining, perhaps therapy, perhaps drugs, perhaps behaviour modification. Whatever it was, it remained under the control of the psychologists. They did not share their expertise with their clients. But new waves of therapeutic techniques grew up alongside each classical school. Alongside psychoanalysis, for example, grew the client-centred therapy of Carl Rogers (Rogers, 1957). He focused on the clients' own ideas of what was wrong and how they might hope to change. The behaviour therapies, which previously had been carried out by therapists, who administered rewards, regimes of punishments and other outcomes of the behaviour to be changed (or, if not they, those in charge of the 'management' of the client), began to evolve

4

into strategies for self-management. These strategies are a kind of do-it-yourself therapy, but like other do-it-yourself activities require clients to acquire new skills. The skills in question involve sharper and more systematized techniques of self-observation, self-control, self-reinforcement. The modification of self and of the environment was to be under the control of the client. These techniques may have been practised unwittingly by everybody since time began, and may look suspiciously like 'common sense' to the casual reader. But a closer look at many self-management therapies will show that they involve highly improved models of common sense, where above all the clients learn to be keenly sensitive to whether or not their actions are resulting in the changes that they have planned. It is in this newer tradition that we find social-skills training – that is training in improving one's encounters with other people.

The change of focus has been brought about partly by the acknowledgement that no therapy can be successful without the active involvement of the clients, and that the greatest influence on anyone is, in the end, themselves. But, as we have said, it was also brought about by the recognition that the clients' own theories about themselves and other people are informing their behaviour, and therefore what is required is a dialogue between two psychologists, one whose ideas have not yet been clearly articulated, an ordinary person as client, and another whose ideas have been articulated, namely, the professional. The dialogue may take many forms. One form is that of offering clients, if they want it, some scientific slants on the processes with which they are concerned, either popularized or in their original published form.

One thing we must remember, though, is that clients and observers of any status have at their disposal very different information about clients' behaviour. The latter cannot experience themselves as others experience them, they need therefore rather specialized feedback about their own reactions. As we shall see later, feedback is a critical element in social-skills training. Although clients have perhaps more information about their lives and behaviour, an observer may see patterns and repetitions in their lives and relationships which the clients do not, simply because their attention is taken up with the details of a crisis, which obscure its similarity to other events that have happened to them. The professional psychologist, therefore, not only has a role as a discussant, in the sense of offering new ways of thinking and perceiving, but also as an important additional source of information to clients about the impact of their behaviour on others. This type of feedback is even more powerful in groups than in individual training – because of the varied perspectives available. These points will be expanded further in the later sections of the book.

Let us attempt a summary at this point. The complex and ambiguous relationship between psychology as science and psychology as practised by everybody has been presented at some length because a fair proportion of social psychology as a discipline is currently concerned with the psychology of everybody (and appears here in particular in chapter 6 on person perception and in chapter 7 on the self-concept). Consequently, when we come to strategies for improving social behaviour, it will be clear in what ways clients are already as much practitioners as their professional counterparts are – even if their practice needs improvement. If we begin with an appreciation of this basic relationship we shall be better able to profit from the real if modest techniques and insights of scientific social psychology.

This first chapter, then, has expressed the basic framework and attitude of present-day social psychologists towards their discipline. In the following chapters we shall be introducing the content of some parts of that discipline – those concerned with social interaction. In chapter 2 we are going to attempt that most difficult of scientific tasks – that of observing our most mundane and taken-for-granted experience, our daily encounters with other people. It is relatively easy to bring into focus the curiosities of mental life, like sexual fetishes, strange fears, deviant social and religious groups with odd beliefs and weird practices, but very difficult to bring into focus everyday behaviour. The Chinese have a saying, 'The fish is the last to discover water', and similarly we have been late to discover everyday life with other people. In the next chapter we shall attempt to do so.

Armed with the works of one of the virtuosos of social science, Erving Goffman, we will extricate ourselves from our participation in everyday encounters and observe from a decent scientific distance that domain which, in his words, 'contains family meals, weddings, chaired meetings, forced marches, service encounters, queues, crowds and couples' (Goffman, 1971, p. 13), to name but a few. As one might watch an ant heap and come to find patterns in what first appeared random and meaningless, patterns which are not visible to the participants as they go about intent on their business, so shall we observe, in this next chapter, social interaction.

2

The structure and goals of social interaction – a cool view

When we study social interaction we are studying for the most part our everyday encounters with other people. Goffman has pointed out that the boundaries of the field have still not been marked out. He subtitled one of his books on the subject *Micro-studies of the Public Order* (Goffman, 1971). This is a useful beginning since it focuses our attention on one of the most interesting features of social interaction, namely its orderliness. Many of our encounters with others seem to run as if we were behaving according to certain rules of procedure. Let us look at this order.

The structure of social interaction

The mere presence of others introduces a degree of control over our demeanour that we do not display when we are alone. We maintain our faces in a moderately expressionless state neither smiling too broadly nor scowling. As we walk, our gait and general body movements are restricted to certain patterns, and we sustain speeds appropriate for the social setting. From strangers we maintain a proper distance and take care not to follow hard on their heels or to remain alongside them. If we inadvertently touch them both parties will usually apologize. Our glances at them are (in our culture) brief and expressionless. Now imagine someone failing to observe any one of these rules. Perhaps they scowl intermittently or grin broadly even though not with anybody. Or they make odd gestures as they walk or swing their arms with the vigour of someone in a walking race. Perhaps they stand motionless, or walk on the extreme edge of the pavement, at an exaggerated distance from other pedestrians, or walk almost touching them. Any one of these items of behaviour would suffice to brand such an actor as at best very eccentric, at worst mentally deranged; in either case as someone to be avoided as a potential source of embarrassment. This control over demeanour suggests we follow quite strict sets of rules of conduct. Yet, ask anyone for the rules regarding proximity to others, say, or facial expression, and they will be unable to specify them. No one has taught us these detailed rules of conduct, yet we observe them. We are in fact quite unaware of their existence until someone does something 'odd'.

Entering into a conversation with someone similarly involves highly regularized sequences. First there has to be some kind of glance exchange (as when one 'catches the eye' of a waiter to get him to the table). Only when one knows someone rather well is it permissible to sidle alongside and to start talking to them without the initial visual permission. This glance is usually followed up with a mutual exchange of smiles, and the person who initiated the encounter is expected to provide the topic of conversation. Encounters most often start with the following sequence:

'Hello.'
'Hello.'
'How are you?'
'Fine, how are you?'
'Fine.'

Then the initiator provides a topic for talk.

Once embarked on the conversation the participants will take it in turns to talk, with few long gaps between remarks or overlaps, where both parties speak simultaneously. The listener will keep up a flow of small head nods, facial expressions and glances. When the speaker gives the listener the eye signal the latter will take the conversational floor and continue the conversational theme, or carefully 'fade' to another theme, or, if he or she wishes to talk about something else, provide some additional signal to that effect. 'By the way' or 'incidentally' function as phrases which cue in a change of subject. Expressions of feeling will be suitable to the topic, and the listener will be observed to maintain a flow of frowns of commiseration and smiles of congratulation where appropriate. Above all both parties will display their attentiveness to the common focus of interest. This is the small change of a million everyday encounters, yet we are again unaware of its orderly quality until someone deviates in even quite minor ways from the rules.

Imagine now some acquaintance who starts to speak in a loud voice without turning towards you or looking at you at all. Or who, to the ritual 'How are you?', begins 'Well, at this point in my life I feel. . . .' Try a conversation in which a friend speaks of the growing traffic problems in the city and you reply with remarks about your aunt's new tea set. Imagine a partner in conversation who stared unblinkingly into your eyes or at your mouth, or waited for ninety seconds before replying to your last, quite mundane remark. Once again any one of these diversions from the rules of conduct is discomforting and signals some kind of mental aberration. Once again, we cannot recall having been taught any of the rules involved, nor indeed are we able to verbalize them.

Ending a conversation elegantly is an art, which anyone who isn't very good at it will willingly admit. The problem is to make it appear that both parties had miraculously and simultaneously hit on the same moment to withdraw from the encounter. Only young, unschooled children will simply stop talking, turn on their heels and just walk off with no expressions of goodwill and regardless of their partner's behaviour. So what usually happens? Schegloff and Sacks (1973), who have observed and recorded samples of conversations in natural settings, have found that, regardless of the content or purpose of a conversation, its final sequences follow a fairly set pattern. There are two stages. The first stage concerns the agreement to close the conversation. One party indicates by some verbal device that the topic has run dry (it is likely that they will be giving non-verbal signals about this too; for example they may speak more slowly, avert their gaze from the listener or decrease proximity). Verbally, however, they will use some common device like: 'Well anyway, that's how things are for the moment', or 'Anyway, things are not too bad/looking up/very difficult', or 'Well, I'm glad to hear it's going well', or 'Yes, that's how it is these days'. If the listener does not accept the invitation to close then they will branch off on some other road offered by the topic. If they do accept it then both parties move on to stage two, which Schegloff and Sacks call 'closure'. This simply involves all the modes of saying goodbye. It includes, aside from actual words, smiles, decreases of proximity, increases of looking, until both parties finally turn their backs and walk off. Schegloff and Sacks point out that if the second party does not accept the agreement to close in stage one, and introduces a new topic, they usually use a special little verbal marker (such as 'by the way' or 'incidentally') as a 'justification'.

These examples of some of the most basic components of any type of interaction should focus attention both on the complexity and also on the orderliness of such interactions. As we shall see in chapter 3, different kinds of social occasion each have their own *implicit* rules of conduct. To repeat, then, one task of the social psychologist is that of uncovering the order that underlies 'family meals, weddings, chaired meetings, forced marches, service encounters, queues, crowds and couples' (Goffman, 1971, p. 13).

There are other, *explicit* rules of social interaction with which we are more familiar, and these rules are known as etiquette. The reason we call them explicit is that somewhere they are written down and if we don't know them already (and want to) we can look them up. They include such things as: how people will address one another, who will sit next to whom at formal dinners, public behaviour between males and females, correct dress, the organization of food and of cutlery to eat it with, a host of details specific to particular groups in society at any given time. Who generates these rules and for what purpose is a fascinating study in its own right. One thing we should remember, however, is that even if we think we are completely 'informal' and 'loose', and the explicit rules of etiquette minimally observable, the hidden etiquette of implicit rules can nevertheless be detectable to the sharp observer.

One might add that societies and groups vary in their 'tightness' or 'looseness', in Goffman's words, and places and occasions vary in the degree to which they call forth rules of demeanour. For example public parks and squares seem to be places where one may loosen control over such behavioural elements as posture, gait, and speed of walking. Whereas inauguration ceremonies, first meals between new in-laws and other such occasions seem relatively 'tight' (Goffman, 1963).

So far we have focused on the fact that social interaction displays an orderly quality and is governed by implicit as well as explicit rules. By focusing on these qualities we have been looking at social interaction in terms of its *structure*. Since the structural approach is an important contribution to social psychology, it is worth spending a few sentences on the meaning of the word 'structural'.

Linguists study a language from a structural point of view. That means that rather than interesting themselves in individual uses of language, their meaning or purpose, they interest themselves in how, as a system, it is patterned. Thus they identify its basic components – sounds, words or morphemes – and the rules which appear to underly the combining of these elements and their recombining to produce sentences – sentences which are intelligible to any native speaker of that language, even if they have not heard any particular one before.

When we study social interaction from a structural point of view, we too try to isolate the basic elements, and these, as we have seen, may range in size from eye blinks and smiles to whole sequences of body movements, as in posture, and whole sentences and sequences, as in greeting and farewell rituals. Once we have isolated the basic components, like the grammarian, we look at the ways in which they are patterned, or rule-following. Students of social interaction are not nearly as far advanced in their study as their colleagues the linguists are. They are far from having identified with precision either the basic elements of interaction or the rules which underlie their patternings, and as observers of social behaviour we still occupy the position of sharp-eyed lay people.

We can make a distinction between the structural approach on the one hand and the functional approach on the other. To come back to language, we can on the one hand look at how language is composed of elements and at the rules behind the combinations of elements; and on the other hand we can look at what function language fulfils, that is what is achieved when people talk to each other, or what it is they are trying to achieve. We find that via language people control one another, persuade one another, pass on information which changes the way others think, build imaginary worlds by speculating, hypothesizing and lying, change their own states of knowledge by asking questions, and so forth.

Can we identify some general functions of the kinds of sequences of interaction described earlier in this chapter? Once again we can turn to Goffman for some suggestions. In his various works he has suggested the following functions: to reduce unpredictability in public behaviour by maintaining 'normal appearances'; to control intimacy and accessibility of people to each other; to indicate the social structure of social occasions; to maintain positive affect and control aggression and hostility; to present and maintain an identity, or self. Let us look at these in more detail.

Goals in social interaction

Normal appearances

One continuing theme in social behaviour is that of the human need for predictability. The vast and complex repertoire of behaviours available to us implies that humans could be extremely unpredictable. The patterned nature of social interaction shows that on the whole it is not unpredictable. Predictable sequences of events are ones that we do not need to pay much attention to, thus freeing our mental resources for tasks which are unpredictable in their outcome, or tasks which are complex. At a meeting, for example, we debate the rights and wrongs of issues and the likely outcomes of decisions, and so forth. We don't have to discuss whether or not we will talk only one at a time, or whether we will stick to the topic being discussed or rather make random remarks about the furniture. This is established already by implicit rules. This means that, with normal appearances maintained, we can use our resources for new or complex tasks. When we maintain normal appearances, others do not have to attend to us in any detailed way. Goffman points out how frequently spies and criminals deflect people's vigilance and attention, in order to cover up their deviant activities, by utilizing their knowledge of what constitutes normal appearances. We all know apocryphal stories of burglars who steal the contents of houses by acting like removal men or by other forms of 'acting normally'. One reason why small departures from normal behaviour are disturbing and lead to the offenders being labelled crazy is that we need our attention freed from this basic scanning in order to concentrate on more complex matters.

Control of intimacy and accessibility

A second major problem in any kind of social interaction is for the actors to control their accessibility to one another. As we already know, people signal their availability or non-availability for social interaction, the levels of intimacy likely to be achieved, and they do so in both psychological and physical terms. Both in public and in less public situations we set up physical and psychological boundaries around ourselves. Physically we keep a spatial zone around us by moving away or closer to others, by avoiding or seeking physical contact and by touching in both ritualized and in informal ways. Psychologically we maintain boundaries around us by limiting the information about ourselves. For example we may allow most people to know what jobs we do, or which part of the city we live in, fewer people to know how we feel about political questions, and very few indeed to know how we feel about close emotional or sexual relationships. We control, to the best of our capacity, the information which is given off in public and which may form the basis of others' impressions of us. By the same token we can increase intimacy by moving towards others both physically and psychologically.

Indicating the social structure of social occasions

This third dimension is concerned with what Goffman calls 'the organization of gatherings'. When people are together in public they signal by various means whom they are with at any particular moment. For example, if you take an aerial photograph of a garden party, it is quite clear that people are organized into dyads and groups. These groups are quite clear, even though the density of the occasion may be such as to make sheer proximity no indicator at all of who is with whom. People manage this by positioning their bodies in particular ways and orienting themselves to others, by the inclines of their heads and trunks, by adopting congruent postures or not, and so forth. Even in a queue it is usually relatively easy to see who is 'with' whom by the position of their heads as they begin to speak. For example, two people who arrived together will talk in a queue without bothering to face one another, two who did not, and who do not know each other, will feel obliged to face one other. A couple on a date will often link arms or hold hands, or use some equivalent 'tie-sign', in public, when they might not have bothered to do so had they been alone (Goffman, 1971).

All this data feeds into our understanding of the social networks around us and allows us to orientate ourselves to people as individuals, as couples or as groups.

Maintenance of positive relations

Affability is more common in our interactions with others than open hostility and conflict. It is rare to see people in open dispute in public places, and unveiled hostility and aggression is usually reserved for the privacy of the family. But this affability has to be worked at. Goffman has suggested that a lot of our interactions with others are ritual exchanges designed for maintaining relationships in a good state. He has described two sorts: supportive interchanges and remedial interchanges (or interactions, to stick to our own terminology).

Supportive interchanges consist of polite queries about health and other concerns, congratulations and commiserations about one's life events and general state of well-being. We do much more of it than we generally realize. These interchanges 'ratify' the good state of the relationship or, to use Goffman's terms, they keep relationships in a proper state of repair (Goffman, 1971).

Remedial interchanges, on the other hand, are concerned with the fact that the relationship is not in a proper state of repair, or, more commonly, is threatened. They involve such verbal devices as: 'I'm sorry', 'I didn't mean', 'If you don't mind my saying so', 'To be perfectly frank', and 'You'll hate me for saying this'. All these are oils for soothing wounded feelings, or for anaesthetizing feelings which may be affronted by what is to follow. Some of Goffman's most telling examples of remedial exchanges concern the rituals surrounding greetings and farewells. He argues that sheer absence is one source of threat to the well-being of a relationship. We recognize this possibility implicitly and ameliorate its effects by nicely correlating the elaborateness of our

15

greetings and farewells with the time elapsing or the distance being travelled (i.e. the amount of 'damage' being done). For example, if we expect to meet a friend again tomorrow, we will bid them goodbye at the front door. If they are off to the other side of the world for an unspecified period we will probably at least go to the airport terminal, if not to the airport itself. If it is a case of 'off to the country for a few weeks', then a prolonged waving until the car disappears may be the proper response. Similarly, greeting a friend after some years demands more than a wave and a smiled 'Hello'; it demands a longish chat, surprised and 'pleased' tones of voice and maybe eating together. Conversely, a nod will do if we have been separated only for a few hours, and even that may be dispensed with if we each keep on popping up. And so it is for effusive embraces, handshakings, speeches, receptions, presents and farewell parties.

Presentation of identity

Finally there is the dimension concerned with the presentation of one's self or identity, both when one is in public and when one is interacting. Self-presentation involves at least two important components. One is the controlling of information that is available to others about oneself in order to give an impression of one's character. One major way in which we do this is by the manipulation of appearances, using cosmetics, clothes and artefacts and props of many sorts. The other component involves claims to a particular role during interaction. To explain this component more clearly it is useful to employ the metaphor of the theatre. The smooth running of a scene in a play on the stage depends on the actors playing their parts adequately. For example, in the bedroom scene in *Hamlet*, Gertrude's shame is meaningless without Hamlet's denunciations. Or, put Mary Poppins into the middle of the storm scene of *King Lear* and everything grinds to a halt. Now, if we think of plays off stage it must be clear that the joker needs someone to laugh, the expert, someone to listen and to be impressed, the seducer, someone to be seduced, the helper, someone who needs help, and so on. It is strange how often we laugh at unfunny jokes, attend to information we don't need or want, allow ourselves to be seduced by people we do not find attractive, and so forth.

Why do we do it? Because the show (in this case the social occasion) must go on. Goffman argues that smooth social interactions depend on the participants each creating for themselves roles or identities, getting others to 'play up' to these roles and everyone playing their parts in credible ways. One major piece of evidence for this idea derives from the phenomenon of embarrassment (Goffman, 1956). Unpleasant and contagious, embarrassment only arises in company. A universal phenomenon, its effects are to cause people extreme psychological discomfort and to bring interactions to an agonized halt until someone exercises 'tact'. It has been suggested (Gross and Stone, 1964) that the most common cause of embarrassment is the failure of someone to carry off the identity that they had been projecting, and on which the identities of everyone else present had been resting. Failure occurs because information discrediting the identity becomes visible to everyone present. The self-proclaimed expert on law shows ignorance of some elementary point or principle. The joker's joke falls flat. Stage actors or musicians forget their lines or make a mess of their performances in a way that cannot be ignored. These failures do not just affect the discredited participant but everyone else present, because the roles or identities we have been playing have, without our knowing it, been predicated on the roles and identities others were playing. How do we go on being an audience when the performer fails? How can one be a pupil to an illiterate teacher, a rebellious teenager to a parent without moral standards? Thus it is argued that social interaction depends critically on people taking up parts or identities *vis-à-vis* one another, backing up their own claims and supporting as far as possible those of other people. That is why we laugh at unfunny jokes and buy things from salesmen when we don't really want to.

Definitions of social interaction

So far we have described the orderly qualities of social interaction and the purposes that lie behind this orderliness. But we haven't given a definition of 'social interaction', and usually the first task is to provide a formal definition of the phenomenon to be discussed. Goffman, who admits that the boundaries of the field have yet to be explored, offers the following: 'It is that class of events which occurs during co-presence and by virtue of co-presence. The ultimate behavioural materials are the glances, gestures, position-ings and verbal statements that people feed into the situation, whether intended or not' (Goffman, 1967, p. 1). Later he distin-guished two levels of interaction, co-presence and focused inter-action.

Co-presence is in fact the minimal level. By this term he means, as suggested in the description given above, that people are co-present when they signal through bodily and facial demeanour, the use of space or any other means, their awareness of one another's presence and their accessibility to one another should the circumstances arise. A good example of this minimal level of interaction, called co-presence, is that found when a group of people are in a waiting room in an incipient queue, as in a doctor's surgery. They will signal their co-presence by slightly adjusting their seating positions with each new arrival, by respecting the queue by deferential nods and even queries, by small conspira-torial smiles to each other if an animal or a child attracts the collective attention, and so forth. But this interaction remains minimal because there is no co-operative action to sustain some joint focus of attention, which, say, a game of snooker, watching television or having a conversation would induce. Co-presence is a minimal kind of interaction but it displays two features: one is that people are monitoring and controlling their own behaviour, as they always do in public but not in private; the other is that they are monitoring the behaviour of others and adjusting their own behaviour accordingly. The non-verbal behaviours have to be recognized and understood, and hence they display that orderly quality mentioned before.

The other level of social interaction, focused interaction, occurs when people gather together and co-operate to sustain a single focus of attention, as in conversations, games, transactions in shops, consultations and a myriad of other social situations. This is what we, as lay people, commonly think of as social interaction. Its upper boundaries are far from clear, however. For example a few people might throw an all-night party, and spend quite a lot of that time drifting about the house or dozing off in one another's presence; whether one refers to the whole episode as a focused gathering or not isn't clear. Similarly, a couple might spend a fortnight in one another's exclusive company on holiday, yet the situation seems to have some features which make it different from focused gatherings in general. There is unfortunately no elegant solution at the present time to this problem of drawing boundaries and providing definitions.

Goffman points out that frequently we participate in co-presence and focused gatherings simultaneously. For example, in a surgery waiting-room one may be 'with' someone and perhaps sharing their magazine or holding a conversation. However, at the same time one would be co-present to the others in the waiting-room, and therefore some slight part of one's behaviour would be directed towards monitoring those present, and adjusting one's behaviour accordingly while still sustaining the focused interaction with the person one had arrived with (Goffman, 1963).

This book is concerned ultimately with ways of improving one's encounters with others, which is what is meant by social skills. For this reason we shall be concerned more with focused interaction than with co-presence. But it should not be forgotten that awareness of co-presence is important. In public we give off many signals to others with whom we may subsequently interact. Through these signals others form impressions of us, which may have important effects on our subsequent relationships with them. Certainly they signal our availability for interaction and likely mood during it. Part of social-skills training involves teaching people to monitor and control the information they give off to others more positively and more effectively.

Summary

Let us now summarize. Social interaction at any level displays an orderly and patterned quality which suggests the presence of implicit rules as well as explicit ones. This order appears in the fulfilment of a number of functions: maintaining normal appearances; controlling access to self; indicating the social structure of social occasions; the maintenance of positive relationships; the presentation of identity.

In this chapter the impression given of social interaction may well have been that of an active dynamic process, with participants using the rules for particular purposes in their own particular styles. But, in fact, a lot of the materials for social interaction are not created by us as we go along, in a form of improvised drama. They are already there. We do not have to invent situations like jumble sales, coffee mornings, love scenes. They already exist with scripts and scenarios long before we come on to the stage. Similarly, many social roles like boss, mother, playboy or policeman are pre-fabricated. Finally social roles and social situations occur against a backdrop – the physical environment – which again we to an extent inherit. In the next chapter we will examine this inheritance in some detail.

3

Roles, situations and environment – the backdrop of social interaction

Human beings are both prisoners of their social and physical environments and creators of them, and a social psychologist has to look at social behaviour from both perspectives: on the one hand, the situations and roles that people create individually and co-operatively, and on the other hand, the roles and situations and institutions which exist prior to any particular person's existence and which influence and constrain his or her experience and behaviour. In this chapter we are going to concern ourselves with the latter.

There are many aspects of cultures which exist before we were born and will continue after death, cultural features which affect profoundly the way we think and act. For example, our language embodies certain features of the world, and not others, and influences our ideas and perceptions. Our feelings about sexual relationships, even today, are influenced by a Christian ideology which predates us by many hundreds of years. In this chapter we will look at three aspects of our culture which affect our interactions with others and which are supra-individual in the sense just described. These three aspects are social roles, social situations and the physical environment.

Social roles

In the last chapter it was asserted that the creation and main-tenance of a role or identity is a critical component of social interaction, and failures in this regard produce embarrassment and damage interaction. These roles or identities are ones which individuals create for themselves during their encounters with others and which are sustained in collusion with them. In this chapter we are going to look at roles which exist independently of any particular individual occupying them. Many social roles are universal because they derive directly from the components of social structure that are universal. Occupation, kinship, gender, age are principles of organization in all societies; that is, people's activities and interests are patterned by such principles. Thus mother, father, sister, brother are universal social roles which derive from the kinship system. Teacher, doctor, nurse, judge are occupational roles which, if not universal, are very widespread. The roles of child and old person, of male and female, since biologically given, are again universal principles of social structure or social organization. What is a social role?

First, social roles are slots or positions in social systems, slots that exist for anyone to occupy and are independent of any particular occupants. Football teams consist of a set of positions which simply require players to occupy them. The second and most important aspects of role positions, however, is that expecta-tions exist about the behaviour of the occupants. For example, the expectations of the centre-forward, or the goalkeeper, or the left-back in a game of football are quite precise, and the indi-viduals occupying those positions will feel obliged to fulfil those expectations to the best of their abilities. We expect, indeed demand, that mothers will ensure the physical well-being of their children, that fathers will support their families financially, that managing directors will take responsibility for the conduct of affairs in their firms, that doctors will use their expertise to try and cure their patients, and so on. Finally, there is of course the actual behaviour of the role occupant, since no two centre-forwards, doctors or mothers behave in exactly identical fashion. So far we have identified three components of social roles, the role position itself, the expectations about the behaviour of an occupant and the actual behaviour of any particular occupant.

Social roles do not exist in isolation; they constitute social systems or role sets. Any occupant of a social role will have role partners, that is, the other members of the role set. The role of husband is predicated on the existence of the role of wife, the role of son on the role of parent, teacher on pupil, patient on doctor, and so on. In a school we have sets of roles which are all interrelated: parents, pupils, governors, teachers, head, caretaker, etc. Each role partner will have particular expectations about another role occupant in the role set. For example, the school caretaker will probably expect the headteacher to organize the financial aspects of keeping the school clean and in good repair. The parents will expect the head to choose new staff and to make sure that the teachers conduct themselves properly. The teachers will expect the head to represent their interests to the local education authority, and the children will expect the head to exercise authority over them.

It should be clear from this exposition that the occupation of a social role can be a major determinant of one's behaviour and experience, and therefore of the type and quality of one's interactions with others. Let us pursue this exposition a bit further and see how roles vary in the demands they make on their occupants and their potential for creating conflict and strain in a social system.

First we have to remember that social roles vary in the degree to which they extend in time and place. For example, the bus conductor steps out of his role when he leaves the bus and the bus station, but the role of mother, particularly if the role partners are very young, is continuous in its demands. Then, roles vary in the degree to which the role expectations involve large sectors of a person's behaviour. For example, the role of nun or priest entails that the occupant be devout, non-materialistic and concerned with the moral dimensions of life all the time and with all people. The expectations of these roles are much more likely to invade the personality of an occupant than are those of librarians or road-workers, whose role demands cease when they go off duty.

Role expectations vary, too, in the degree to which they are formally prescribed and sanctioned. A mother is required legally to maintain her child's physical well-being, to the best of her ability, and if she does not, she may be summoned and imprisoned for neglect; however, it is not formally laid down that she has to play with her child, or read it stories. With most roles there is some central expectation which is prescribed, sanctionable and agreed on by other role partners, and peripheral expectations which are implicit, at the discretion of the occupant and not necessarily agreed upon by all role partners.

Role expectations also vary in the degree of precision with which they are coded. Hospital nurses know precisely what they have to do on the ward at particular points during the day. The role has specified that by a particular hour all patients will have been washed and had their beds made and medications administered. The role of 'poet in residence' at a university, however, carries few specifications as to how the occupant should spend any particular portion of the day; how many poems have to be written during the term of residence is certainly not written into the contract!

However, a social system, whether a family, a school, a university department or a firm, rarely works perfectly. Roles can easily come into conflict, causing role strain for the role occupants, which will affect behaviour and ultimately undermine the functioning of that system. Role strain means simply that the role occupant feels some psychological discomfort associated with the role.

If role expectations are not sufficiently clear to guide one's behaviour and interactions with others, one will suffer the psychological discomfort of not knowing how to act. Nurses working in psychiatric hospitals have been found to suffer this discomfort when the focus of the organization has changed and therefore their role within it. When, for example, their previously specified custodial role was partially removed in a new 'therapeutic community', and no very precise duties substituted (Schwarz, 1957), they would suffer the anxiety of not knowing what they were supposed to do in any particular contingency.

Sometimes the various role partners have expectations of a role occupant that directly conflict with one another. For example, school governors might expect economies to be the top priority of the head; teachers or parents, however, might expect extra spending. The head cannot please both. Couples can enter into marriage and, regardless of their individual dispositions and feelings towards each other, experience role conflict and the accompanying role strain because their expectations of each others' roles are not in accord. The wife might expect the husband to make all the decisions about their joint finances, whereas he expects them to share this responsibility. He might expect to organize his social life without reference to her, whereas she expects to play a role in his plans.

Then, people rarely occupy only one role at a time. Many people are spouses, parents, offspring, employees, friends, secretaries of clubs or political parties, or occupy whatever voluntary roles they may fancy. If the expectations associated with all these roles are conflicting and are present at the same time and in the same place, individuals will feel the strain of not knowing how to allocate priorities and the pressures of others expecting them to act decisively. A woman in full-time employment may have some very important assignment at work exactly when her child falls ill. A man may have his father, who has always dominated him, staying in his house with his own children, over whom he exercises a lot of authority. His submissive role with his father will not accord with his dominating role with his own children. The result in such cases is that of confusion in the individual about how to act.

All these sources of role strain arise largely out of the malfunctioning of a system rather than out of the specific qualities of the individual. A coherent, unconflicting role system has not been developed either because it is new, as in the case of a new post or job being created but not fully worked out, or because a system has changed in its nature.

There are sources of role strain, however, which may derive from the lack of the qualities in the individual necessary to fulfil the role expectations. Some women who are not easily nurturers nevertheless become mothers. Timid, compliant people may, through circumstances, find themselves temporarily in positions of leadership and authority. People with high moral standards may find themselves forced at work to choose between two equally unsavoury courses of action. But even with these sources of conflict, where some part resides within the individual, another part resides outside the individual, in a system or context.

Role conflict and role strain that arise out of the malfunctioning of social systems can be considered to be the counterpart of the embarrassment which signals the malfunctioning of the improvised roles or identities we create in interaction with others. Both phenomena draw attention to the degree to which our experiences with others are socially created and not simply a product of our personalities or other psychological characteristics.

It should be clear at this point that a fair portion of our interactions with others can be understood in terms of social roles, which we do not individually create, and in terms of conflicts in role systems which are more a product of the system than of the individuals occupying them at any particular time. It is necessary to consider, when we have problems in our relationships and interactions with others, whether these problems can be resolved by examining them from the perspective of role theory.

Where does the individual enter, then, in this perspective? Earlier on in this chapter a distinction was made between role expectations and the actual behaviour of any occupant at a particular time. No two individuals play out role expectations in identical ways. To a degree, roles are created anew by their occupants, and with varying degrees of originality. The resources for this originality come from within particular individuals and, popularized, may transform the conventions for playing that role. The tomboy mother, the politically radical priest, the globe-trotting grandparents have had to be created and popularized before becoming part of the recognized modes of playing these roles. And individuals with their particular personalities will have created them.

One final point must be mentioned. Roles do not entail just behavioural expectations; they also entail norms and stereotypes. Many of the expectations that we have of roles develop a moral quality. This is particularly clear when we think about some more general roles generated by age and gender. It feels to us morally wrong for people to behave like teenagers once they are middle-aged, and the sight of a middle-aged person regularly frequenting a disco for teenagers is likely to call forth a moral response, not couched in terms of the rights and wrongs of their actions (since probably little harm will have been done by the behaviour) so much as their 'stability' or 'immaturity', which are the more usual ways in which we express moral judgements these days. Similarly we would question the healthy development of a little girl who wore fur coats and jewellery, regularly read *The Times* and never went out to play. Equally pervasive are the stereotypes of masculinity and femininity which many people hold. For example they may expect males to be more effective in some situations, like motoring, and females to be more effective in other situations, like dealing with social functions.

Many of the more specific roles have stereotypes associated with them. We expect bank managers and chartered accountants to be different kinds of people to rock musicians and social workers (and indeed they often are, but how far such differences are a product of social expectations rather than arising out of 'real' differences is not clear). We expect older people to be more conservative in their general attitudes than the young (although this frequently is not the case). Space is reserved elsewhere in the book (pp. 92–3) for looking more closely at social stereotypes, but they are mentioned here to reinforce the argument that the processes associated with recognized social roles have an important impact on our behaviour and experience and therefore on our interaction with other people.

Social situations

Like social roles and identities, social situations can be regarded as being created by individuals during their interactions with others. On the other hand they can also be regarded as existing independently of any participant or set of participants. Like social roles, we can view social situations as scenarios awaiting actors to bring them to life. Let us consider for a moment the former perspective.

One group of social psychologists and sociologists, the symbolic interactionists, have always stressed that it is the actors' definition of a situation, rather than its objective properties, observable to the outsider, that has consequences for behaviour and experience in that situation (Thomas and Thomas, 1928). For example, a dinner party given for friends and colleagues may be defined by them and by observers as an informal, and enjoyable, social event. However, the adolescent son, who is also present, may define the situation to himself as one which has been set up to test his social skills and for that reason it may feel to him more like an officer-selection exercise than an informal social occasion. A student invited to the home of a supervisor may find that the situation has elements which appear to reflect the latter's definition of it as a seduction scene. Individuals define situations for themselves, and these definitions have an impact on how they behave.

Symbolic interactionists suggest, furthermore, that many definitions of situations are actually arrived at through the process of interaction itself. According to this view, participants co-operate to sustain a particular definition of the situation, in the same way as they co-operate to support each other's projection of an identity and thus prevent embarrassment (Ball, 1970a). We have all come across situations, like works outings or family Christmas parties, where everyone acts up to try and sustain the definition of the event as one of unmitigated fun, regardless of contradictory features which are apparent to the observer. Ball (1967) noted that in the waiting-rooms of abortion clinics, situations which for many might still have some residual associations with unsavoury and illegal activities, much of the activity of the personnel is given over to sustaining an atmosphere of extreme medical respectability. Weinberg (1965) has similarly observed how in nudist colonies, where observers or initiates might read some sexual definition of the situation, participants 'work' hard to neutralize such a reading and, by their 'clothed' glances and carefully restrained physical contact, define their situation in terms of love of nature rather than a sexual free-for-all. Whether social situation exists solely in the head of an individual participant or is created by participants in collusion with one another, both perspectives suggest that the objective and quantifiable features of social situations are not really very significant in their impact on the individual.

The second perspective suggests that situations *do* exist independently of individuals in them, and that their objective characteristics have important consequences. No particular individual creates such social events as jumble sales, seminars, transactions over shop counters, choir rehearsals, and the like, yet they have a sizeable effect on the way people behave in them and how they interact with one another. The feelings expressed, the general emotional tone, the clothes worn, the amount of physical contact, even the 'tightness' of one's posture depends on the situation one is in. Several psychologists have argued that there are many features of everyday situations which are construed very similarly by any group of people, that is that most people think of, say, coffee mornings or formal interviews in very similar ways, and that the personal and subjective nature of the definition of the situation has been over-stressed (Argyle *et al.*, 1981).

As soon as we embark on an *objective* study of social situation, however, we have a number of problems. The first one is that the list of social situations which can differentially affect social interaction is infinite. We are confronted with the same problem that we met in the study of social interaction in general, that the term 'social situation' has no conceptual boundaries to it, and we have not agreed upon a definition of what a social situation is.

Perhaps the first task is that of classifying social situations in terms of shared and differentiating features. For example we might classify situations in terms of the domains in which they occur – domestic, occupational, social, leisure, commercial, religious, etc. Or we might classify them in terms of the relationships between the participants – formal, intimate, competitive, co-operative. The difficulty with any such scheme is that there will always be situations that do not fit into any one category. Furthermore there will always be disagreements between people about where particular situations belong. For example, playing football or the piano are leisure activities to the amateur, but they are occupational activities to the professional. Anyway, classifying situations on an intuitive basis still does not provide us with a formal definition of what a situation is. Unfortunately the formal definitions available are not very precise. Consider the following:

a place with its surroundings that is occupied by something. *(Oxford English Dictionary)*

A general term for the field of reference (stimuli, objects, fellow man, groups, values, etc.). (Eysenck *et al.*, 1972)

By the term social situation I shall refer to the full spatial environment anywhere within which an entering person becomes a member of the gathering that is (or does then become) present. Situations begin when mutual monitoring occurs and lapse when the next to last person has left. (Goffman, 1961)

This last, the reader will observe, sounds like the definitions of co-presence considered in the previous chapter. These formal definitions do not bring us as close to an appreciation of what social situations are as does our lay person's understanding of the term. Since theoretical work on social situations seems to have arrived at a cul-de-sac, let us look at some empirical work on identifying and classifying social situations. One approach in this line has been that of Forgas (1976). Rather than simply using his own intuitions about the nature of social situations and how they might be classified, Forgas used his sample of subjects to do so. That is, the task of identifying social situations was an empirical rather than a speculative one. Situations are what a group of people, collectively, think they are. He brought together two groups of subjects, housewives and university students. He asked all of them to give a detailed account of their interactions during the previous twenty-four hours, and to list other usually recurring activities which happened not to have occurred during that period. They were also asked to give two adjectives describing each interaction. Thus Forgas, instead of thinking up situations out of his own intuitions (which might be very particular to him), took a sample from a group which he hoped might be a representative sample of a population. At the very least one might suppose that they were representative samples of housewives and university students.

Forgas selected (having eliminated repeats) the twenty-three most frequently occurring situations mentioned by each group, plus one or two others that were interesting but not so frequent. He then had two lists of common episodes. The next task was that of identifying the properties which either differentiated or linked them. Once again he could have generated his own conceptual scheme, but instead, wishing to find out how they were generally classified, he went back to his subjects with each situation written on a card. He asked them to compare the situations and to put them into groups according to their similarity with one another, allowing the subjects to use their own dimensions for their judgements of similarity. He now had the groupings of all the situations by all the subjects. He then used a special technique, called multi-dimensional scaling (Rosenberg and Sedlak 1972), to represent in a space the closeness or similarity of the situations to one another. The space can be multi-dimensional and in this particular study was three-dimensional and was pictured as a cube with situations inside it. Figure 1 shows the cube that was constructed for the student sample and gives the list of situations the students classified according to their similarity.

From the cube represented in figure 1 we can see that all the situations which the subjects had grouped were to do with

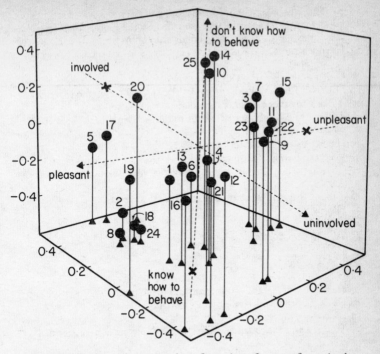

Figure 1 The three-dimensional configuration of twenty-five episodes: student sample

The twenty-five most frequently mentioned social episodes for each sub-sample:

Housewives (n = 25)

1 Having a short chat with the delivery man.
2 Playing with your children.
3 Your husband rings up from work to discuss something.
4 Having a short chat with the shop assistant while shopping.
5 Having dinner with your family.
6 Shopping at the supermarket on Saturday morning with your husband.
7 Attending a wedding.
8 Having a drink with some friends in the pub.
9 Washing up dishes after dinner with family help.
10 Chatting over morning coffee with some friends.

11 Reading and talking in bed before going to sleep.
12 Chatting with an acquaintance who unexpectedly gives you a lift.
13 Watching television with your family after dinner.
14 Having a short chat with an acquaintance you unexpectedly meet on the street.
15 Going to the pictures with some friends.
16 Discussing the events of the day with your husband in the evening.
17 Talking to other customers while queueing in a shop.
18 Talking to a neighbour who calls to borrow some household equipment.
19 Having guests for dinner.
20 Visiting a friend in hospital.
21 Chatting with others while waiting for your washing in the coin laundry.
22 Talking to a neighbour through the backyard fence.
23 Playing chess.
24 Going to the bank.
25 Visiting your doctor.

Students (n = 23)

1 Having morning coffee with people in the department.
2 Having a drink with some friends in a pub.
3 Discussing an essay during a tutorial.
4 Meeting an acquaintance while checking your pigeonhole for mail in college.
5 Going out for a walk with a friend.
6 Shopping at the supermarket on Saturday morning with a friend.
7 Acting as a subject in a psychology experiment.
8 Going to the pictures with some friends.
9 Having a short chat with the shop assistant while shopping.
10 Getting acquainted with a new person during dinner in hall.
11 Going to junior-common-room meetings.
12 Chatting with an acquaintance before a lecture begins.
13 Discussing psychology topics with friends.
14 Meeting new people at a sherry party in college.
15 Visiting your doctor.
16 Chatting with an acquaintance who unexpectedly gives you a lift.
17 Visiting a friend in his college room.
18 Going to see a play at the theatre with friends.
19 Going to the bank.
20 Having an intimate conversation with your boy/girlfriend.
21 Having a short chat with an acquaintance you unexpectedly meet in the street.

22 Chatting with others while waiting for your washing in the coin laundry.
23 Attending a wedding.
24 Watching television with some friends.
25 Playing chess.

Scales derived from adjectives provided by subjects

involved – uninvolved
simple – complex
active – passive
pleasant – unpleasant
intimate – non-intimate
very much at ease – very ill at ease
know how to behave – don't know how to behave
friendly – unfriendly
occasional – regular
organized – disorganized
co-operative – competitive
formal – informal

Source: Forgas, 1976 (© 1976 American Psychological Association.
Reprinted/adapted by permission of the publisher and author.)

---

involvement, pleasantness and knowing how to behave – features of the situations which relate to the subjective experiences of the participants. 'Knowing how to behave' presumably refers to knowledge of the rules of behaviour in situations, a feature which we have already identified in social interaction.

One of the most important features of this study is the technique used. For with this procedure we could select many samples of populations and compare the situations which they provide. Furthermore we could compare the ways in which different groups of people construe the same situations. And we could begin to see from the labels the subjects gave to their groupings what were for them the *critical* features of social situations. Those critical features would be ones that would impinge most on the individuals' behaviour and experience. The technique of multi-dimensional scaling permits us to uncover some collective definitions of situations. However, one can see that the technique could also be used for studying the recurring definitions of situations by particular individuals. Thus individuals could both provide lists of situations and group them according to similarity.

Individuals' dimensions, uncovered by the analysis, would represent their *subjective* definitions of situations, which the symbolic interactionists believe to be so important.

Other researchers have examined directly people's perceptions of rules in social situations. For example, in one study subjects were shown some of the situations produced in the Forgas study just described, given pairs of these situations and asked to differentiate between them on the basis of rules which would apply to the one and not to the other. The rules were both prescriptive and proscriptive. Some 124 rules were obtained using this procedure. Some of the rules elicited in this manner were general rules, for example about being friendly and positive to other people; others were quite specific, for example about smartness of dress on particular occasions, about the avoidance of gloomy topics of conversation, about following others' advice and directions, and so forth. The researchers found no difficulty in getting subjects to verbalize rules and found a considerable degree of agreement between them on what the rules were. It was thus possible also to classify situations in terms of shared or differentiating rules (Argyle *et al.*, 1979).

An alternative approach to the study of the implicit rules of social situations has been that of Garfinkel (1967). Termed 'ethnomethodology', it involved the researchers in 'invading' a real-life situation and violating what was felt to be an important underlying rule sustaining it. For example, they might attempt to haggle about the price of items at the check-out point in a supermarket or behave like honoured guests in their own homes by requesting to use the bathroom or to have a glass of water. Or they might query some taken-for-granted pieces of information exchange, as in the following sequence:

A I had a flat tyre on the way here.
B What do you *mean* you had a flat tyre?

The ensuing consternation and suspicion of the innocent participants was evidence that the violation had indeed been of a critical nature.

It must by now be clear to the reader that psychological research in this area is still at a very early stage. Given the clear importance of social situations for constraining behaviour, this delay in progress needs some explanation.

Until recently, psychologists, with one or two notable exceptions such as Barker in his work on ecological psychology (1968), had ignored the effects of context on behaviour. In their search for universal laws of behaviour, that is behaviour which remains constant across time and place, they conducted their research within the confines of the psychological laboratory. The psychological laboratory is of course one kind of social situation, but only one, and a pretty unusual one at that.

In the laboratory psychologists try to construct replicas of elements in situations as they believe them to occur in everyday life. For example they might be interested in the effects of stress on behaviour or performance. In such a case they might select one supposedly stress-producing factor, like noise or overcrowding, something they think can be measured and controlled, and then contrive to isolate its effects on behaviour. But there are several problems with this approach. First neither of these variables can really be measured. Sound can be measured, but noise is a subjective response to sound and depends on individual attitudes. Density can be measured, but overcrowding is density experienced together with other variables, like its anticipated duration, its reasons for existing, the nature of the other people present. Then, under normal conditions neither of these variables operates alone. For example both may be associated with poverty, insecurity and poor health. Their effects, in a word, depend on the context in which they are experienced and therefore this context must be studied.

The reason for this neglect of the situation lies very much in the efforts of psychologists to maintain psychology as an exact science practised in the laboratory where precise quantification is the major goal. The experimental technique is part of that endeavour.

Another effect of this bias has been the search for factors *internal* to individuals as the major explanation for their actions, one of these factors being personality. Personality appears to lend itself to quantification and considerable research effort has gone into the construction of tests to measure it, the assumption being that a score, or profile of scores, would enable one to predict the person's behaviour, regardless of the situation. It is only relatively recently that it has been appreciated how much behaviour varies as a function of the *situation*. Consequently psychologists have had to return to a preliminary stage of enquiry, with situation now as the target of study.

Physical environment

We have looked at the shaping of social behaviour that can be traced to the influence of the social environment, that is roles and situations. Now we turn to the physical environment.

The term 'physical environment' covers many different types of variable. It includes such variables as climate and terrain, urban versus rural settings, agents of stress like noise and crowding, house layouts, furniture arrangements. This wide range and diversity of variables means that we are going to have to be very selective in the choice we make for discussion. Since the focus of this book is on the modification of interpersonal behaviour, the discussion will be restricted to those factors which are modifiable. Thus, although a factor like climate exercises a powerful influence on patterns of social interaction (for example a warm, temperate climate leads to outdoor living and therefore enhances sociability, in contrast to a cold damp climate), it will not be discussed, because we can't change the weather.

Restricting the discussion to modifiable features of the environment is a reminder that, as with social roles and situations, we can consider the physical environment both as a dependent variable (that is it is created by people and expresses many aspects of social life) and as an independent variable (that is it exists independently of the humans who occupy it and has an effect on their behaviour).

Then one must remember that although the physical environment can be objectified and quantified, its effects are mediated partially through people's perception of it. Take noise as an example. We can quantify sound very precisely. We cannot specify with the same precision when sound will became noise. Noise is unwanted sound. Whether it is wanted or not depends on the listener's tastes and attitudes. A baby crying and a dog barking may produce the same number of decibels but be perceived very differently according to whether one likes dogs or babies. Because of the importance of these interpretive processes, one important concern of environmental psychology is that of how people construe their environments.

In this section the discussion will focus on the way in which the physical environment can affect social interactions, with regard to the following: facilitating or impeding social interaction; privacy and the maintenance of boundaries around the self; expressing the social structure of gatherings; defining the situation; and influencing the emotional tone of interactions.

Facilitating or impeding social interaction

People tend to choose friends from amongst those with whom they interact frequently (Homans, 1961). The built environment can have a powerful influence on the ease and frequency with which we encounter other people. A number of studies of housing complexes illustrate the point. In one study (Festinger *et al.*, 1950) it was found that people living in flats next to the central stairwell received more friendship nominations than people in other positions along the corridor. People whose flats faced the street rather than the courtyard received fewer friendship nominations than other people. The authors drew a distinction between linear distance and functional distance. Linear distance is simply the physical distance between two front doors; functional distance is produced by positioning which affects opportunities for chance contacts. Both were found to have some effect on friendship choices, but other research on housing and friendship networks have found functional distance to be the more important. In one study (Athanasiou and Yoshioka, 1973) of a suburban housing estate it was found that housewives visited neighbours across the street more often than they visited neighbours next door, whom in turn they visited more than backyard neighbours. All the houses had more windows in the front, and all the main entrances and driveways were in the front. This suggests that the sheer visibility of others is a factor in generating interaction. A number of studies have suggested that the string-like nature of the average suburban environment does not favour casual contact in the way some urban slum environments have. Courtyards, steps where people can sit out closely enough to hold conversations in the open air, small shops close to dwellings – all these features facilitate informal contact because they provide communal as opposed to privatized space.

We find similar factors operating if we move indoors. Chairs in lines or rows inhibit interaction, partly because they restrict the opportunity for eye contact and other visual feedback which plays such an important role in managing conversations. Any teacher will confirm that creating discussion between members of a class is very hard while the pupils remain seated in rows. Open-plan arrangements in schools and offices tend to produce less interaction than the more traditional closed spaces (Brookes and Kaplan, 1972). Spatial layout is not the only feature of the physical environment which can enhance or minimize social interaction. Levels and types of noise can have dramatic effects. High levels of background noise, apart from sometimes causing hearing loss, inhibit conversation. This is largely because of the effort needed to raise one's voice above the background noise, and the fact that raising one's voice increases the general level of noise. Not only that, conversing under noisy conditions forces people to be physically closer than they might want or the situation might warrant, and also produces bodily orientations which limit visual feedback. Furthermore, noise is a form of over-stimulation and the desire to reduce this level will inhibit the desire to interact.

Milgram (1970) has claimed that city living produces many forms of over-stimulation, of which noise is just one. First, densities in cities are greater than in urban or suburban areas, and this means that an individual not only encounters many more people in a day, but many more different people most of whom will not be seen again. Great varieties of activities and scenes add to the stimulation, or over-stimulation, of the city environment. Milgram argues that the need to reduce stimulation leads to distinctive patterns of interaction. People are more likely to be ignored even if they ask for help, and to be dealt with more hurriedly and impersonally if they are not ignored. Certainly Milgram's own research showed reluctance to interact by urban as opposed to small-town dwellers.

Privacy and the maintenance of boundaries around the self

Privacy is a state in which one has control over other people's access to one's person or information about one's person. Most people have two potentially opposing needs: one is to be available to others for social contact; the other is to have privacy. Some people need more privacy, others more social contact. If we think about the environment, whether at the level of public spaces or domestic spaces, we can see features which reflect these two needs. In western society the door is a ubiquitous architectural feature, and curtains are almost obligatory parts of our domestic props. The possibility of closing or opening doors and curtains is a device for signalling availability. Goffman (1959) has drawn attention to the prevalence of back (private) regions and front (public) regions both in domestic settings and in public settings. Back regions, which in houses include bedrooms, bathrooms and sometimes kitchens, are regions in which only intimates may penetrate without invitation. Front regions are open to the public. He also points out the existence of arm rests marking off the territories between seats in theatres and trains, and the use of swivel seats (in the US) on public vehicles which enable people to avoid eye contact if not physical proximity. In fact the environment can be considered entirely from a territorial point of view, where the major distinction is between public and personal spaces. Where the territorial markings are inadequate, as in many institutions, inmates will use their own markers, usually personal possessions, to retain control over the territory.

Environmental psychologists distinguish between two concepts concerned with the use of space: personal space refers to the invisible buffer zone that one carries around everywhere, that surrounds the body; and territoriality refers to fixed regions which individuals claim as theirs and defend against invasion. Environments can be arranged to facilitate both types of boundary maintenance. Restaurants which become popular for reasons other than the food and service are often designed to allow for both privacy and accessibility. There will be a public area, usually centrally placed with many tables and public corridors between them where one can see and be seen and approached; and there will also be alcoves, or at least tables surrounded by some kind of barrier (Goffman (1971) calls these 'stalls'), in which individuals or couples can set themselves apart from the public territory. One can see the same kind of phenomenon on camping sites. People arriving early and staying long will claim a space in a corner, or with some kind of boundary marker; indeed, often the proprietor will mark spaces out quite precisely. Latecomers and those moving on will be allocated the open unmarked spaces in the middle of the site, and be subjected to inadvertent invasions of their privacy. Parties too are more enjoyable if held in rooms or houses with both types of space available.

Goffman has pointed out the widespread relationship between power and rank on the one hand, and the size both of buffer zones and territory which the individual is permitted on the other. The more important the person (in a social sense) the less others are permitted to approach him closely, speak of him within earshot, and the greater the size and number of areas which he is permitted to control. Probably one of the most trying features of poverty is the lack of privacy that is typical of the living conditions of the poor and the public institutions allocated to them (Goffman, 1971).

Expressing the social structure of gatherings

The relationship between the size of territory one is permitted to control, and one's social rank, brings us to the next relationship between environment and social interaction, that of environment and social structure. The two dimensions of social structure most obviously symbolized by the layout of the buildings concern relationships of solidarity on the one hand, and relationships based on status differential on the other – the horizontal versus the vertical principles in social structure (Brown, 1965). The clearest examples of this symbolism can be found in buildings whose functions have a strong element of ritual in them. Churches and temples pertaining to many religions show clearly from their layout alone the fact that participants contain an élite, or a leader, who occupies a particular part of the building, this part usually being elevated. In Christian churches, for example, there is a pulpit and altar, strongly illuminated either by a concentration of windows or special lighting, for the priest, and the undifferentiated spaces of the nave which the congregation occupy. When religious movements split up into factions, the radical ones are often committed to breaking up the hierarchy and the distinctions between priests and communicants. This is quickly reflected in their buildings by a reduction in status markers like raised areas and barriers. Lecture halls, schools and rooms arranged for firms' dinners, all show these basic features.

Work places and many other public buildings often have two

types of door: the first type will be at the front of the building, often at the top of some steps, usually wider and taller than is required to admit one person. The other type of door is usually to be found at the back or edge of a building, on the level with the ground, and is clearly person-sized. These doors are not used equally by all occupants of the building, the large one being reserved for persons of special status.

Inside public buildings status arrangements abound. Buffer zones, in the form of ante-rooms, waiting-rooms, secretaries' rooms, protect the high-ranking occupant from the masses. On entering such a complex, one will be aware that very particular kinds of interaction are about to ensue, with the high-ranking occupant being privileged to choose the moment for the interaction to start, the topic to be addressed and the moment for it to end.

The room laid out and ready for the wedding party will typically indicate the social structure of the occasion which is about to take place. For example there will be one table which is obviously reserved for the closest kin of the couple; from the number of places set we can see how many of them there are. There may be one or two others of intermediate size, which look as though they are reserved for more distant kin and close friends. Then there will be long tables for lots of people, or many identical tables for (in relationship terms) identical people.

Restaurants for different ethnic groups neatly suggest the favoured groupings for eating out in a particular culture. On normal occasions Anglo-Saxons do not eat in large groups (they do few things in large groups). The standard table is laid for four, suggesting the average family, or the two-couple outing. Greek restaurants, on the other hand, often have very large tables indeed, suggesting that they go around in larger groups, both of un-related people in the community and of extended kin groups. Chinese restaurants also indicate larger groups and in addition often use round tables and present the food in communal bowls.

These arrangements alert us to the social structure of the occasion, who is 'with' whom, the fundamental networks and divisions, and allow us to prepare ourselves for particular types of interaction.

Most of us are aware that certain types of environmental setting are 'appropriate' for certain activities. Some of the environmental components which add to the suitability of a setting for an activity have a functional relationship with that activity. For example it is obvious that a laboratory is designed for particular activities to be carried out in it. However, just as many components render a setting 'appropriate' on the basis of their meaning or symbolic value. For example it would be very much more difficult to carry off a romantic encounter in a room full of gunmetal-grey furniture, with strip-lighting, bare linoleum and shelves filled with back copies of the *Builders' Gazette*, than it would be in most sitting-rooms, even if in the former the necessary components of privacy and seating were ensured. But this is so because of what these props *mean*, what they symbolize to us – not because in reality they affect the encounter at all. Therefore when we create situations we often modify the environment to create the right atmosphere. A person giving an informal party will put cushions on the floor rather than provide extra chairs, leave on display evidence of other activities like knitting or typewriters; a person giving a formal party will soften the lighting, get rid of the television, make some effort to segregate activities like eating and talking or dancing and provide more marked-out spaces. The monochrome working environments for adults and the crowded, colourful infant-school classroom proclaim the assumptions underlying the situations which are enacted in each place and how the actors are supposed to feel in each place. Whether functional or symbolic, environmental components support the definition of the situation.

Research has shown that people will alter the layout of chairs and tables according to the situation they are trying to achieve. Casual conversations and co-operation in a task lead them to favour side-by-side arrangements. A competitive situation favours participants taking up positions opposite each other. Taking the dominant role in a meeting leads the occupant to take up a position giving maximum visibility of the other participants (Sommer, 1969). The importance of room arrangement for expressing the situation will be appreciated when one learns that at the Paris peace conference at the end of the Vietnam war it took ten weeks to achieve table arrangements which reflected to everyone's satisfaction the political status of the participants, in particular, of course, the positioning of the National Liberation Front delegates and the representatives of the South Vietnamese government (Kitchens, 1974). Very often the environment can be manipulated to mask the true definition of the situation. An interview for a job, or place on a course, may be held in an elegant study, followed up with a stroll around the rose garden, while all the time the conversation may be allowed to 'stray' across a variety of topics. On the other hand it can take place in a gunmetal setting, the applicants queuing up in an unseemly line in a dirty corridor outside the office. The competition in the former situation is probably more cut-throat than in the latter, but the 'atmosphere' generated by the setting may mislead the applicants into thinking otherwise.

The close link between environmental setting and social behaviour is demonstrated in studies of the behaviour of people in closed institutions. In one study, for example, the researchers examined the effects of the introduction of carpeting into the wards of a public mental hospital. They found the following: reduction of incontinence; quieter talk and more modulated behaviour, patients being considerably less irritable and excitable; reduction of injuries and accidents. The bleakness and squalor of many institutional buildings carry strong messages about the role the inmates are expected to play, and the fact that very often they fulfil these expectations has often been taken as evidence to justify the continuation of such environments.

Influencing the emotional tone of interactions

The environment plays some role in modulating our emotional responses to other people. This has already been suggested by Milgram's work (1970) on city environments and over-stimulation mentioned in a previous section of this chapter. The exposure to too many different people in an environment reduces the volume and diversity of our responses to them. Crowding in a closed environment can produce even stronger negative effects. Crowding, like noise, results in part from an interpretative process and is not simply a function of the density of people in a given area. People experience high density as crowding if they cannot control it, if the other people are strangers, if it is likely to be prolonged,

43

and so forth. It is difficult to obtain evidence on the effects of crowding on responses to other people, because in real life crowding is usually compounded with other noxious environmental variables, like poverty, ill-health and noise. However, where these factors have been equated, it has been found that people in high-density situations express less favourable reactions to the others present (Nogami, 1976). There are a number of possible reasons for this. One is that high density does heighten arousal, which in some situations (like carnivals or football matches) might be experienced as pleasurable but in others, for example work situations, could be unpleasant and lead to hostility to others present. A second reason is that high density reduces the potential for individuals to regulate their proximity to others, and therefore they will be unable to sustain their preferred level of personal space and thus control the access of others to them. A third reason is that crowded environments usually entail a competition for resources, for example, in slums, access to water and toilet facilities. Thus a setting where resources are scarce will mean continual frustration of the individual's goals, this frustration leading to hostility.

Another environmental factor that has been examined with respect to its effects on interaction is the emotional and aesthetic qualities of a setting. Modern urban environments are, for the most part, very ugly and we have few resources available to us as individuals to modify them or to avoid them. Inside these built environments we do have and do exercise a degree of control.

We must ask what is meant by terms such as 'ugly' or 'attractive'. Like noise or crowding, the aesthetic value attached to any stimulus must lie in the mind of the beholder. Yet we have some evidence that people evaluate environments in similar ways, and Berlyne (1971) has suggested some objectifiable features of any visual composition which would lead to its being preferred on aesthetic criteria.

In one study subjects were presented with a series of line drawings of rooms. The researchers systematically varied certain components, such as ceiling-slope angle (i.e. sloping or horizontal), window shapes and positions, numbers of alcoves, and arrangement of seating and rugs. The subjects were asked to rate the rooms on such dimensions as 'harmony', 'friendliness' and comfort. Figure 2 shows the rooms rated as 'most friendly' and

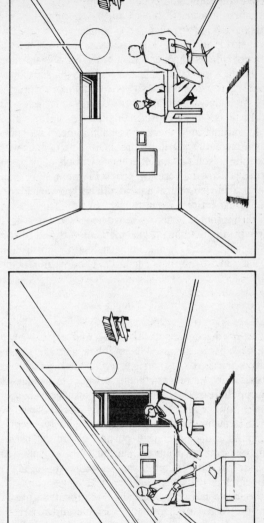

Figure 2 A 'friendly' and an 'unfriendly' room

Source: Wools and Canter, 1970 (reproduced by permission of Butterworths).

'least friendly'. They found that ceiling slope and seating arrangements carried most weight in positive evaluations.

Having demonstrated that people do evaluate the qualities of a setting in similar ways, we can go on to enquire whether this evaluation has any effect on interpersonal processes. An early study by Maslow and Mintz (1956) showed that subjects judged photographs of other people and of themselves less favourably if the judgement task took place in an 'ugly' room than if it took place in an 'attractive' room. Mintz also discovered that interviews did not last as long in ugly rooms as they did in attractive ones. All this suggests (but does not do more than suggest) that the aesthetic qualities of a setting could have an impact on people's emotional responses to one another and on their actual behaviour with one another. Aesthetic settings are of course symbols of social status, and the possession of beautiful props in the way of valuable furniture and pictures are a sign of wealth and power. This factor alone could be expected to exert an influence on people's perceptions of one another. Certainly most people manipulate their domestic environments both for aesthetic effects and to enhance their status, probably as lay psychologists, with the intuition that this may have benefits for their encounters and relationships with others.

Summary

In this chapter three aspects of contextual effects on social interaction have been examined. First it has been shown that the social environment is partially structured through social roles and role systems which derive from the structure of the wider society, and the occupation of these roles has an influence on the individual's behaviour with others. Secondly social situations or episodes also determine certain features of social interaction, and these situations are common to particular groups in society. Thirdly the physical environment can facilitate or impede many features of social interaction, from its basic frequency to its emotional quality.

Throughout we have stressed the reciprocal nature of the relationship between any contextual variable and interaction or behaviour. People are constrained by factors they did not create, but they modify and recreate the settings and roles and in so doing gain some control over their interactions and relationships with others. Thus the context can be seen as an independent variable or as a dependent variable, depending on the focus of the research which is being carried out.

4

Communication, language and social interaction

Of social interaction Goffman writes the following: 'It is that class of events which occurs during co-presence and by virtue of co-presence. The ultimate behavioural materials are the glances, gestures, positionings and verbal statements that people feed into the situation, whether intended or not' (Goffman, 1967, p. 1). This last sentence reminds us that interaction consists of communication. In this and the following chapter we shall examine in more detail the resources and systems that comprise our modes of communication.

Simple systems of communication often possess the following features:

1 Every message has a sender and a receiver, both of whom are fully aware of the message.
2 Every message will be in one particular code or medium.
3 Both sender and receiver who understands the code receive the message identically.
4 Everyone understanding the code understands the message

since its meaning is invariant, regardless of the circumstances or the identities of the sender and receiver.

Morse code is a system that has these features. Each element has one invariant meaning, and whether the message is sent by an admiral or a boy scout, from the top of a mountain or the middle of the ocean, in fair weather or foul, its meaning remains constant.

Human communication could hardly be more different. In the first place we communicate with language, with our bodies and with all the artefacts with which our environment is rich. Thus we have at least three media of communication, which may operate independently of one another or interact (and most of the time we do not know which). Secondly both as senders and as receivers we are often only partially aware of messages we are sending or messages to which we are responding. Usually we are aware of and intend verbal messages, but not, for example, hand movements or changes in posture. Thirdly there is much communal meaning to our words, gestures and props, but there is also as much which is not communal. My meaning for 'friendship' or 'luxury' may not be at all the same as yours. Your frown may mean disapproval to one person, but puzzlement to another. Her casual clothes carry no special meaning for her, but to them they signal deliberate unconventionality. Fourthly most of the meaning of a message can only be understood with reference to the context or situation in which it occurs. For example the words 'double fault' make sense only in the context of a game of tennis; walking along with a piece of white cloth on a stick makes sense only in the context of warfare; a raised eyebrow on the part of a teacher has a meaning peculiar to the classroom. Fifthly (as will be discussed in the final chapter) humans often carry the context around in their heads, and the meanings of a message cannot be understood without knowledge of what the sender and receiver already know. Consider the following pair of sentences, the second being a response to the first:

SON Both John and Trevor have cars.
FATHER I am very hard up at the moment.

The first sentence can be understood as a request for a car, and the second sentence as a refusal, but it is possible that only the participants will connect the two statements. Similarly 'It is hot in here', 'Do you think we could have the window open', 'Aren't these rooms stuffy' are all alternative forms to 'Open the window'. Which one is chosen depends on contextual features. Linguistic elements are symbols. A symbol is an arbitrary sign for something. Symbols only come to stand for the things that they do, because a community of symbol-users agree that they shall. Neither the sound, nor the appearance of the word 'shop', for example, bears any resemblance to what it represents, but our collective agreement on the class of things to which the word may refer provides that symbol with its use for communication purposes. A different collection of people might use it slightly differently. For them the word might refer also to small workshops where goods are repaired and spare parts sold, to open backs of lorries and to the kinds of trestles or barrows that we call stalls.

The fact that symbols emerge through some kind of social process to represent reality in a particular way has a number of implications. One of these is that the 'real world' may not be experienced directly at all; it is a reality socially constructed through symbol designation. Another is that we learn that a symbol can evoke in another person's mind the same response that it does in our own; thus we can imagine their mental reactions and anticipate their responses and on that basis choose courses of action.

However, because of the highly contingent way in which our symbols relate to the 'world out there' and to our intentions and other psychological states, communication often breaks down, and we fail to understand one another. Consequently, although we have the capacity to anticipate the responses of others to the symbols we use, we can also be wrong. The task for everyone is to get a clearer understanding of their communications to other people, and of the messages that they send. The task of the social scientist is that of gaining a formal understanding of how our different modes of communication are used, how they relate to each other, to situation and to user, and to understand the lay person's understanding of communications.

Let us begin by considering language because that is the system whose formal properties are, at the moment, best understood. The case of language constitutes a good example of where the study of human social behaviour benefits from a multi-disciplinary perspective. Our formal understanding of language derives from work in descriptive linguistics. The framework that linguistics has provided for understanding language gives us a point of comparison for the study of other communication systems, where our knowledge of their structure is considerably less advanced. We will now look briefly at language as a structured system.

Language

We experience speech as a continuous stream of sound, just as we experience body movement as an undifferentiated sequence or flow. However, in the case of language, even with those languages which are not written, linguists can segment this stream into discrete elements which combine and recombine according to rules of grammar or syntax. Thus language consists of a finite set of elements and a finite set of rules for combining elements. This characteristic gives the system two important qualities: one is *redundancy* and the other *generative power*. Redundancy in the system means that there exists more information than is actually needed for understanding the message. In the sentence 'Please sit down, dixxer is sexxxd', a number of letters have become defaced (if the sentence were spoken we might imagine that loud noise obliterated the sound of the speaker's voice at those moments). However, all native speakers of English can supply the defaced items from their implicit knowledge, or competence, concerning English syntax. From both the existing letters and the preceding words, and from the non-linguistic context too, listeners have sufficient information to understand the message. Those items are therefore redundant. The redundancy of language allows it to remain an effective system in 'noisy' conditions – conditions in which people's use of it is idiosyncratic, where the environment is actually noisy and listening conditions restricted, and so forth.

The generative power refers to the fact that the system allows for the creation of new elements and therefore new messages. New words come into a language like English daily, and new sentences are being born every moment which are instantly understood by listeners who have never heard those particular sentences before. As culture, technology and society evolve, language evolves too.

Language: its structure

The smallest elements which are usable for constructing units of meaning are phonetic segments. Each language has its own phonetic alphabet which is simply a sub-sample of all the sounds which can be made by the human articulatory apparatus. These phonetic segments combine to create morphemes. However, they combine according to certain rules. In English, for example, we do not find a morphemic segment beginning with the following combinations of consonants: *zd*, *pf*, *ts*, *hl*. But in other languages they can be found. We rarely terminate an English morphemic segment with a voiced vowel, but in Italian nearly all terminate in this way. Therefore at a glance we can know whether a word is an English word or not, and furthermore we know whether it could ever possibly be an English word. Contrast *sprode* and *sfandla*. The first is not at present, but could become, an English word; the second could not. Through such constraints phonetic segments are synthesized into morphemes. The morpheme, or morphemic segment, is the smallest unit which carries meaning, and is often smaller than a word. The following word has three morphemes: *un-kind-ly*. *Kind* is a free morpheme, it can stand alone and its meaning can be found in the dictionary. *Un* is a bound morpheme, that is, it cannot stand alone and can only modify the meaning of a free morpheme, and usually means some form of negation. *Ly* is another bound morpheme, an example of what linguists call grammatical morphemes. Its function is to change the morpheme to which it is attached into another form class. *Ly* turns a word into an adverb, and so its meaning is 'a mode of doing something'. Morphemes are combined into words, which can be of two types: content words like *apple*, *believe*, *pretty*, *slowly* and function words like *you*, *the*, *more*, *in*, *and*, *because*. Morphemes and words are the building blocks of propositions or ideas, and these in turn are the building blocks of sentences. Examine the following sentence:

The young man, who jumped on the bus, dropped his wallet.

First let us divide it into morphemes:

The young man who jump/ed on the bus dropp/ed his wallet.

Now let us divide it into propositions, or ideas:

The man was young.
The man jumped on the bus.
The man dropped his wallet.
The wallet was the man's.

and so forth. The rules for combining propositions are numerous and complex, but nevertheless constitute the linguistic competence of normal adults, a competence that for the most part they are unaware of. As with the implicit rules of social interaction, most people find it very difficult to formulate the rules of grammar in their own language but can detect an ungrammatical sentence easily. It is quite beyond the scope of this text to present a grammar, for there are many. Suffice it to say that no full specification of the rules of any language has as yet been completed, although our understanding of the formal properties of language is much more advanced than our understanding of such properties of non-verbal communication.

Grammatical or syntactic rules specify what elements can be combined with what elements, where elements can be deleted, and the linear ordering of them in languages where word order is a critical element. For example such rules could specify a sentence as having the following format:

Sentence = noun phrase + verb phrase
Noun phrase = article + noun + adjective
Verb phrase = verb + noun phrase
noun = man/girl/dog, etc.
article = the/a, etc.
adjective = pretty/happy/friendly, etc.
verb = likes/sees/eats, etc.

Another way of representing it could be:

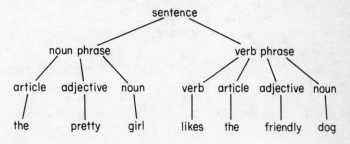

53

This of course represents only a tiny segment of the rules which would be required to generate many different kinds of sentence. These rules account for the speech as it is heard or read, that is the surface structure of a language. Underlying these structures are meanings not necessarily apparent in the structure. The point can be appreciated when one considers two pairs of sentences in which, first, the meaning varies but the surface structure remains constant and, second, the meaning is constant but the surface structure varies.

They are (visiting foreigners).
They (are visiting) foreigners.
The leg was bandaged by the nurse.
The nurse bandaged the leg.

So far we have been talking about the organization of elements within sentences. The term grammar is often thought to refer only to the rules up to this level. However, in recent years a number of people have argued that whole stretches of speech or prose may show regularities of organization which may be called grammar, in this case a grammar of discourse. Take for example the case of stories. Stories (if they are to be more than simply a string of events) have to have a form of organization which relates events, characters and settings. It has to show clearly which items are part of the main plot and which are part of the sub-plot, and so forth. It has been suggested that stories are, like other elements of language, hierarchically organized, each level subsuming the one below it. The elements of a story to be combined, according to Rumelhart (1975) can be represented in the following way:

Story = setting + episode
Episode = event + reaction to event
Event = action or change of state
Reaction = internal response and overt response, etc.

Try fitting some story you know to this scheme.

Explanations, jokes, directions and instructions may also have invariant structures, which take account of the ordering that the listener needs to have in order to comprehend. In all these types of discourse there have to be rules which account for the following:

only grammar but meaning, that is the way in which elements relate to non-linguistic phenomena. Grammar cannot in practice be separated from meaning, but for present purposes one can examine meaning just at the level of individual words.

There are two types of meaning, denotative and connotative. Denotative meaning refers to the features or characteristics which an entity must have in order to qualify for the particular name that a community of language users assign to it. The word 'uncle', for example, will have the following features: living, human, male, brother of either parent or husband of sister of either parent. In another community the word might denote a larger class of entities, or a smaller one. These features comprise the denotative meaning, and that meaning can be represented in a way that allows comparison with other words:

	living	*human*	*male*	*brother of parent, etc.*
uncle	x	x	x	x
aunt	x	x	o	o

However, the denotative meaning of a word may change according to the linguistic context in which it is used, for example: 'charged with theft' and 'charged with looking after the house'. This is why grammar and meaning cannot be separated. Word meanings may vary from one person to another in terms of certain components (this is particularly true of abstract words); nevertheless core meanings can be understood and are of course represented in dictionaries. Denotative meaning has a degree of flexibility in the sense that it can change with use and can acquire different features as a result of being used in particular contexts.

Connotative meaning refers not to the features of a word but to one's reaction to it, that is to its emotional content. The word 'slimy', for example, has a nastier connotation than the word 'silky'. Consider the following two lines of poetry, one being a denotatively equivalent but connotatively contrasting version of the other.

Season of mists and mellow fruitfulness
('Ode to Autumn', Keats)
Time of fog and ripe productivity   (after Wallwork, 1969)

There is nothing objectively or inherently 'poetic' about words like 'mist' or 'mellow', and yet we experience them as strongly so. It is hard to remember that even their pleasant sound qualities are arbitrarily created by social evaluation too. The connotative meaning of words can be measured and represented. One method of doing this is to ask people to rate words in terms of other concepts on bipolar scales:

Poetry
happy/sad
strong/weak
fast/slow

The resulting evaluations for a group of subjects represents the connotative meaning shared by that group. The scale is called a 'semantic differential' (Osgood *et al.*, 1957). Those authors found that subjects rated words in terms of three dimensions of 'affective tone': evaluative (i.e. good–bad), potency (strength) and activity. The good–bad dimension was the most important for distinguishing between words. More complex techniques like the multi-dimensional scaling discussed in chapter 3 have also been used to explore both denotative and connotative meaning simultaneously (Romney *et al.*, 1972).

Words and the entities to which they refer acquire social and emotional value, and it is this value which has the greatest and most insidious power for creating attitudes and reactions in other people and injecting 'atmosphere' into situations. The most obvious examples of the conscious exploitation of the connotative value of words are to be found in advertising and in political propaganda. There we meet euphemisms like conciliation (appeasement), separate development (racial discrimination), dentures (false teeth). We meet the exploitation of connotative meaning in the form of image-building devices like 'dawn-picked' mushrooms, 'midnight' mints, Avenger Mark II, and the like. And we meet them again in such associative engineering as 'From the most distinguished tobacco house in the world – cigarettes by John Player'. ('House' usually refers to a place where individual items like clothes are designed, rather than a factory for mass production. Similarly the word 'by' is usually used in connection with an artist creating say costumes for a stage production.) The manipulation of connotative meaning is clearly a resource in influencing people, in impression management and in defining situations. It is therefore an important aspect of verbal and social skill.

Social context and language choice

Up to this point we have examined the raw materials of language as a system, the assumption being that the form that sentences or discourses take is generated simply by linguistic considerations, that is by the grammatical rules and the semantic fields of individual words and phrases. It is only when we came to the question of connotative meaning that the world outside language made its presence felt.

The fact is that with all these raw materials of language we have enormous choice over the forms that we use, and the factors determining those choices are not linguistic ones but for the most part social and interpersonal. When we speak, we provide those bits of information that are not already provided by the context, or by what we believe the listener to know already. We choose words which have power to persuade; we select registers, or styles of talk which are appropriate to the topic, to the listener and to the situation; we may select accents or terms which give a particular impression of self. Let us look first in more detail at the business of fitting our speech to the listener's state of knowledge and to the gaps left by the context. Even at the level of sentence there is a thematic structure (Halliday, 1970) which reflects our assumptions about what others present need to know. Consider the following statements: 'I have given the sofa to Jennifer' and 'I have given Jennifer the sofa'. From the first statement one would guess that the listener knew about the sofa already, but wanted to know to whom it had been given. In the second the listener seems to know that Jennifer was being given something, the only question being what. Here word order has been chosen to indicate 'given' and 'new' information. The choice depends on the speaker's beliefs about the listener's state of knowledge. The choice of the definite article 'the' as opposed to the indefinite article 'a' is similarly governed by the listener's state of knowledge. When an item is mentioned for the first time in a conversation the indefinite article will be used; for example, 'Go and get a bottle of wine from the cupboard'. Afterwards the bottle of wine will be referred to as 'the': 'Let's open the bottle of wine now'.

Then the level of precision of our choices not only reflects what the listener needs to know but can also set in motion a chain of inference in the listener, as the following piece of humour indicates:

'I saw Fred in a restaurant with a woman yesterday evening.'
'Does his wife know?'
'He was with his wife.'

Thus an important dimension governing our linguistic choices is that concerned with knowledge assumed to be shared, and the degree of linguistic explicitness demanded. A lecture to an unknown audience, with no visual aids, on an abstract or technical topic being introduced for the first time, will require that everything be clearly spelled out. A group of workmen examining the same hole in the road and chatting about it can take a lot for granted. But one must remember that it is extremely rare for any significant portion of speech to be really explicit. The utterance 'Open the door' could be expanded indefinitely, producing such strings as 'Put pressure with one hand on the metal lever to the left of the wooden slab in the wall, pushing it until it moves; by pressure I mean that the muscles of the hand contract', etc. 'Open the door', like most of the things that we say, presumes an enormous amount of shared knowledge. Speech which lies towards the taken-for-granted end of the continuum has been called 'restricted code' and speech at the other end 'elaborated code' (Bernstein, 1966). Whenever we tell a story, or give directions or instructions, we have to select the right point on the continuum of restriction to elaboration. That point will be based on our beliefs about our listeners.

We use forms of address and styles of speech to indicate relationships of status and intimacy between speaker and listener. The formal and informal 'you' in many languages marks out the intimate from the distant, and surnames, Christian names, nicknames and all the epithets like 'love', 'comrade', and 'man' do the same. But we can also distinguish formal and informal styles. For example, there is a world of difference in the following forms of the same invitation: 'Do drop in on us anytime' and 'My husband and I would be delighted if you would pay us a visit sometime'. The difference anticipates the kind of relationship the host and the guest are likely to have.

In English, politeness and formality are often indicated by indirect speech modes. 'Open the window' has a number of forms which increase in politeness and indirectness:

Open the window.
Open the window please.
Would you mind opening the window?
It is awfully stuffy in here, do you think we could possibly have the window ajar, just for a moment?

Asking a person a direct question (for example, 'Where have you been?') may in certain relationships be more hazardous to that relationship than some roundabout mode such as: 'I was wondering where you were' or 'I suppose you have just come from X' (as said by parent to nearly grown-up son).

Language choice at any level not only reflects a situation or set of relationships; it can go some way to creating them. To adopt an informal mode is one way of taking the tension out of any encounter. Using such linguistic 'tags' as 'you know', 'isn't it', 'like' creates a pressure to agreement and accord in the listener. Assuming shared referents can define a situation as one of intimacy or solidarity even before it has been established by any other means. For example, a speaker asks, 'Have you seen the Burne-Jones?' The listeners are far from clear what the Burne-Jones is, but they know that they are being invited to view themselves as people who do. If they reply, 'What's the Burne-Jones?' they will break the 'intimacy spell'. However, if they wait for the conversation to unfold, they will soon find out that Burne-Jones was a painter and there is a current exhibition of his work, and they will find that implicitly they feel themselves to be part of some group of people who have seen it.

Language accommodation and social interaction

One technique for making verbal encounters run more smoothly, which many people adopt, apparently without realizing it, is accommodation. Speakers may attempt to enhance their value for another speaker by drifting towards the other's mode of speech (Giles *et al.*, 1973). This can be at the level of accent, for example a television interviewer drifting towards the cockney of the interviewee. It can be at the level of style, for example, teachers who hope to 'get on' with their pupils may speak about their subjects in exaggeratedly 'inarticulate' styles. It can involve simply the use of some phrase that aspiring social climbers associate with the class to which they would like to belong.

The capacity to modify one's speech, whether at the level of accent or register, to fit in with a situation or a group of people is an important one. Note the word 'capacity' – as with any social skill it is important to have the ability to do something even though one might not choose to exercise that ability. Because of the strong association between language use and social class in Britain, in any situation where an individual is bound to confront people from different classes, the capacity to modify speech needs to be acquired. This is true in teaching, in situations where interviewing is a major component, in management and in supervision.

Language and social status

One dimension of social interaction which is frequently present, but less frequently acknowledged, is that concerned with power and status. One benefit of superior social status is that one is entitled to initiate interaction with lower-status individuals where the latter do not have this right. For example, teachers most often summon pupils, bosses employees, professors the other members of staff. Similarly they can use the intimate or informal mode of address, whereas the lower-status person will remain with the formal one. Once into conversation they will have the right to choose the topic, to ask the questions and decide whether answers are adequate, to change the subject, to butt in and to terminate the whole encounter. This process can be seen most vividly in educational settings between teachers and children, where teachers do almost all the talking, ask questions to which they have answers, decide whether responses are adequate and change the subject with a stunning degree of arbitrariness (Furlong, 1976). However, it is possible to find mild versions of this state of affairs in many everyday encounters, both where some difference of status or power is perceived to exist, or where one participant is making an effort to establish it.

A number of studies have illustrated the process with reference to differences between men and women in their conversational speech style, women, for the most part enjoying inferior status and less power than men. It has been observed that women in conversation use a more 'hesitant' style, as shown by the fact that they ask two or three times as many questions as men and use more of the 'tags' mentioned earlier: 'you know', 'isn't it', 'couldn't we', etc. (Lakoff, 1975). Lakoff argued that the reason for this lay in the way in which women are socialized to be insecure and unassertive. A later study by Fishman (1979) showed quite clearly that the reason for women (or anyone else) using the question mode (given that many questions are not really questions) is that a question is a stronger mode than a declarative since it forces the other to respond. Therefore it is a strategy for getting some control in a conversation which may otherwise falter. In Fishman's study the conversational samples were collected from couples talking to each other at home. The tags were found to cluster around those points in conversations where the woman was getting quite inadequate responses from the men, or the latter were attempting to switch topic. In another study Fishman found that without the question strategy, women had considerably more difficulty than men in getting their topics adopted in conversation. It seemed that a woman had to work harder at a conversation than a man did, especially if she wanted to control the topic. Fishman pointed out that probably the same strategies might be seen in dyads of two males with unequal status. In an experimental study in which dyads (mixed or same sex) had to discuss an issue, and in which one member was given the role of expert by being fed prior information, only men expressed this advantage in a more dominant speech mode. This was indicated by interruptions, overlaps, length of remarks, completion of remarks, as against such assent responses as 'I agree', 'Mm', 'You're right', etc. (Leet-Pellegrini, 1980).

It has been observed that in group training of women, which involves discussion, one of the first tasks is that of getting women to give their opinions directly, without such preambles as 'What I was wondering was . . .' or 'I wonder if I could say something here . . .' or 'I don't know much about this but . . .' and other such 'appeasement' strategies.

Language is perhaps the most powerful resource that we have, and verbal skills are central to social skills. All human languages are extremely complex, as the slight introduction to descriptive

63

linguistics at the beginning of this chapter must have indicated. A fair proportion of this complex system is acquired spontaneously, without special tuition, at an early age, and soon becomes knowledge which is entirely implicit. But a fair proportion does not. Our vocabularies expand throughout life if our experiences are rich and varied. Our use of existing vocabulary and sentence structures can be developed to virtuoso heights. Our appreciation of the power of connotation can always be sharpened. These are basic linguistic skills which should be central in school curricula, because, apart from any other benefits, they are necessary resources for skilled social performance.

Just as important, but less often recognized, is the degree to which the structure of our speech is built on assumptions about the listener's state of mind. Part of social-skills training is teaching people to listen to others, and also to ensure that the inferences they are making, both in their speech and in their heads, are valid and that the meanings that they attach to particular linguistic symbols are the same as those in the minds of other people. This needs special vigilance and special types of awareness. Many professional social skills involve giving instructions and directions; many informal social skills involve telling jokes and stories. All of these verbal activities require planning to produce a structure that is adequate for the listener's needs. It must be clear that skill in these processes also involves perception of others, the interpretation of the feedback that they provide, as well as the cognitive skills involved in planning discourse.

We shall see in the later sections of this book that considerable use has been made of the research on relationships between interpersonal processes, situation and speech in formulating exercises for developing assertive or supportive speech styles, for controlling conversations, for integrating oneself into groups of different types, and so forth. But now we turn to non-verbal communication.

5

Non-verbal communication

Non-verbal communication is communication through any means other than language. Non-verbal communication includes communication through body movement and body posture, gaze, voice qualities, the manipulation of space and the arrangement of environmental props, and personal appearance, in the use of clothing and cosmetics. In fact whole actions and sequences of action can be communicative. For example an individual who makes it his business to be seen in close conversation with a very high-status individual may be communicating to others about his own social value.

Neither language nor non-verbal communication fit the simple model of a communication system presented at the beginning of the last chapter. There are, however, problems of studying non-verbal communication which the study of language does not encounter. First and foremost it has not yet proved possible to provide a structural analysis of non-verbal communication at the level of precision available for language, and therefore we have no systematic framework for its study.

The structure of non-verbal communication

Like language, non-verbal behaviour can be experienced as a continuous, unsegmented stream. Unlike language, with its phonemes, morphemes, words and propositions, each one subsuming the previous one, even units of body language cannot easily be identified. One researcher has attempted for some years to make such an analysis. Birdwhistell (1970) analysed short film segments in order to construct a model of body movement akin to that of language. For example, he isolated elements which he called 'kinemes' – lateral head sweeps, eyelid closures, hand movements, and so forth – which combined into larger units, constructions that formed a stream of communication. However, there is no comparison between the detailed knowledge we have of syntax in language and the fragmentary observations of sequences that have emerged so far from film analyses. And this has been done, anyway, with respect only to body movement. We know nothing at all about the grammar and elements of other types of non-verbal communication. This means that when we look at non-verbal communication, and the roles which it may be playing in social interaction, it is as if we were studying isolated scraps of some linguistic system, never sure if we have a message or only a fragment of a message, or indeed random sound.

Information or communication

Only some non-verbal elements are really communicative. We know that language *always* is because a speaker cannot speak without intending to do so and therefore without an intention to communicate. But a fair amount of body movement may be out of the control of the actor, and caused by factors which have nothing to do with the situation. Clothing and props can be communicative but they are not if they are produced by agents outside the actor. For example dungarees are not communicative in China, any more than a dinner jacket is at an old boys' dinner, because in each case they are the only possible things to wear. Voice qualities can be produced by purely physiological mechanisms or by emotional states, as can body movements. Consequently some behavioural elements are communicative, that is they are transmitted, received and have common codes of meaning for both sender and receiver, and some are simply informative. Head scratching and hand-to-face movements can inform observers about the actor's state of relaxation or tension, although it can tell them nothing more specific and may have no bearing on the immediate situation. However, a smile, a direct look and a quick movement of the eyebrows is a greeting and a signal of availability and readiness to interact. The former is informative; the latter is communicative.

Another problem concerns awareness and control. Many of the most important non-verbal elements of communication, for example those which co-ordinate speech in conversations, lie outside the awareness of both sender and receiver. Blushing is informative; the blusher may be aware of it but unable to control it and certainly not intending to communicate with it. These ambiguities surrounding the interpretation of non-verbal communication are not there, however, simply to make life difficult for the researcher; they are essential to one of the major functions of non-verbal communication, that of dropping hints. Very often people may wish to send messages without committing themselves too strongly to them. For example we may want to indicate our reservations about someone. To do so verbally might well produce effects on that person which we do not want. To do so non-verbally, by tone of voice, avoidance of gaze or any other means, will be a kind of hint which can be retracted later and, most importantly, denied if one so wishes when one's reservations have disappeared. The very ambiguity surrounding the status of non-verbal elements in communication provides social interaction with a high degree of flexibility. This flexibility is somewhat akin to that found in diplomatic exchanges where messages are hedged and guarded and require interpretation. The function is the same, namely that of preserving a relationship, while intimating feelings and intentions which might be unacceptable and in later, improved circumstances be proved unfounded. This diplomatic flexibility exists because we cannot use non-verbal communication as evidence since it may have been out of the control of the sender and outside his awareness. Non-verbal communication is a language adapted for hint and innuendo.

A skilled professional actor acquires the capacity to use non-verbal elements to portray character, emotion, attitudes – elements which for most of us would not be under our control. A stage actor can, for example, weep and laugh to order, make his voice crack with grief or ring with anger. Part of social-skills training is concerned with helping us to become better actors, in the sense of being more aware of and more able to control behaviour which carries messages for others. Similarly, on the receiving end, we can learn to be more aware of and to interpret behaviour of others. Thus, for example, when we are very close to a person we notice changes in facial expression or small movements that a stranger would not notice. Social-skills training is also concerned with teaching us to read others with greater accuracy, even if they are strangers.

These two chapters on communication produce a separation between two modes, the verbal and the non-verbal, which is mostly unjustified because in interaction there is a remarkable synchrony between speech and, for example, body movement (Condon and Ogston, 1967). The separation is partly justified, however, because most psychological research on non-verbal communication has examined the role of isolated elements in interaction. Much psychological research is concerned with providing subjects with non-verbal cues isolated from each other and from speech, and obtaining their judgements of the psychological states being communicated. Nevertheless, despite the gaps in our knowledge concerning the formal structure of non-verbal communication (if it exists), and its status as information, or communication, great progress has been made in understanding the kind of information that it can carry, and this research has provided the basis for many programmes concerned with the development of interpersonal and social skills.

Many elements of non-verbal communication remain relatively stable during social interactions. We communicate a great deal about the nature of the occasion, and about ourselves and the roles we anticipate playing, through clothes, furniture and the arrangement of space, props and artefacts. When we arrive at a party formally dressed we communicate our expectations about the likely nature of the occasion. A teacher coming into a lecture room can either use the raised platform, which will clearly indicate that he or she will do most of the talking, control the topic and take responsibility for ending the encounter, or the teacher can sit in an inconspicuous position amongst the class, which will indicate that everyone present is eligible to participate and to choose the topics. These features are static in that they remain stable for the duration of the encounter, are chosen beforehand and are not really modifiable by anything that happens during the encounter. But these static features are important since they provide information about the definition of the situation and the role structure which will be necessary for the encounter to run smoothly. In chapter 3 we saw how seating arrangements, for example, facilitate different types of interaction, and the material in that chapter provides us with copious information about the static elements of non-verbal communication.

Non-verbal communication – the primitive language

Unlike language, non-verbal communication reminds us of our biological roots and our links with other living species. Some elements of non-verbal communication are biologically determined expressions of emotional responses. These emotional responses are fundamental to survival and to the regulation of our most basic relationships with others. The emotions are those of anger, fear, attraction and the relationships generated through sexuality, parents with offspring, dominance and submission, altruism and co-operation. The elements through which all this is expressed are a primitive part of our behavioural repertoire, the residual elements of behaviour patterns which changed through processes of evolution to become facial expressions, gestures and other body movements. For example, anger in many species involves baring the teeth in preparation for biting. Facial expressions of anger in humans also involve a slight baring and protrusion of the teeth, and suppression of the anger involves compressing the lips. Another example is the eyebrow flash, a universal element in greeting. The eyebrows in humans, and in many kinds of monkey, are marked strongly enough to be used as a signal. In many cultures people use cosmetics to mark the eyebrows even more strongly. They are a flexible and clear signal to conspecifics. Charles Darwin, whose research traced out the evolution of facial expressions from earlier gross behavioural patterns, argued that the head nod, a universal device for refusal, derived from a shaking-off movement found in many species. Kissing, a universal signal of affectionate greeting and affection, generally occurs in chimpanzees too, and derives perhaps from the mouth-to-mouth feeding which is a widespread phenomenon.

These non-verbal signals of emotion and regulators of interaction are instinctive, that is unlearned, and are found amongst people blind from birth and in widely separated cultures. Thus they are universal. Ekman *et al.* (1972) presented people from literate and pre-literate cultures with photographs of faces taken from the same range of cultures. These faces were staged expressions of emotions like happiness, sadness, surprise, anger, disgust and fear. They were recognized with a high degree of accuracy both within and across different cultures. New Guinea highlanders were quite capable of recognizing the expressions of French people as the latter were of Africans, and so on. Then, the ethologist Eibl-Eibesfeldt (1975) has documented the expressive behaviours of peoples from widely differing cultures, using mirror lenses which enabled him to film people without their awareness. These films have shown a great number of behaviour patterns occurring universally in the same contexts. One example concerns the greeting over a short distance. The head is raised slightly, the eyebrows are rapidly raised (the eyebrow flash) and then there is a nod and a smile. Another concerns behaviour of an individual who is slightly bashful or embarrassed. The person alternates looking at and looking away from the person who has accosted him, shows a 'repressed' smile and hides the mouth behind the hand. Eibl-Eibesfeldt interprets this as behaviour which results from a conflict between approach and flight or avoidance.

Physical proximity is an indicator of intimacy, and maintaining physical distance is a mark of deference and distance in all cultures. Staring is a threat, and long looks are a sign of mutual involvement in all cultures. We have a biologically determined repertoire of expressive behaviours which all members of the human species can interpret in the same ways. However, this repertoire is simply a set of raw materials which are *usable*, but not necessarily *used* to the same extent in different cultures. For example, because we have a degree of control over facial expression we can inhibit the display of emotion through this medium. For example, amongst the Japanese the eyebrow flash is inhibited between adults. Many of the Indians of the American Plains maintain control over their facial musculature in order to hide emotional expression. Proximity, which has a universal significance for the intimacy or distance of a relationship, shows great variation in its actual use. People from northern Europe and North America maintain greater amounts of space between themselves and others, at every level of psychological intimacy, than do people from the Middle East. The rules governing expressive gestures originate within the culture, although the gestures themselves are biological in origin.

Deception and the control of non-verbal expressions of emotional states

Unlike other species, humans have a capacity for self-monitoring and, as we have seen, the capacity to minimize the spontaneous expression of feeling to a great extent. This capacity also provides the potential for deception, not found in other species. The latter implies that when we are trying to detect emotional states in others we may have to rely on those cues over which they have less control. Ekman *et al.* (1969) showed films of people who were attempting to conceal some aspects of their psychological states, and found that observers shown only movements of feet and legs, or hands, were more accurate at detecting the real states than those who were shown the faces. The authors called this type of cue to concealed emotional states 'leakage'. Other research has identified other sources of information about concealed emotional states, for example that people who are concealing something make more hand-to-face movements and fiddle with objects (Knapp *et al.*, 1974).

Ekman, Wallace and Friesen point out that the reason that people have less control over some bodily movements than others is simply that they are less accustomed to paying attention to them. For example we are relatively unaware of movements of the feet or hands. Skilled actors, who are taught through direct study with feedback to monitor and control emotional expression in *all* parts of the body, show less 'leakage' than ordinary people do.

This work on leakage brings into focus another interesting point about the expression of feeling through non-verbal channels. If one can conceal feelings, one can, presumably, feign them too. To feign emotions via those expressive movements which are generally believed to be spontaneous and uncontrollable makes one immune to responsibility for them. One can use such a channel for conveying a message about one's feelings while disclaiming the message. This possibility equips the non-verbal channels with a subtlety and flexibility which language, intentional and therefore committing as it is, often lacks. *Expression* of emotion is important not only for detecting the internal states of others during interaction, it is important also for people's experience of it, that is the physical expression of emotion is closely linked to the experience of it. For example a number of studies have shown that people who do *not* inhibit expressions of pain also have lower pain thresholds. In other investigations it has been found that people induced to pose a facial expression of emotion induce the emotion. For example one study suggested that if subjects simply *pose* a smiling face this affects their mood. Laird (1974) induced subjects to smile while they were carrying out the apparently unrelated task of rating funny pictures for their humour. The 'smiling' subjects enhanced their humour ratings of the stimuli. One explanation for this finding runs thus: people are unsure of exactly how they feel, one piece of information which they can use to establish what it is that they are feeling derives from their own behaviour. In this case the subjects might say to themselves, 'I am smiling, and so I must find these pictures funny.' (This account of how we interpret our feelings will be developed in more detail in chapter 7.) People should, then, through deliberate acting, be able to extend some control over their feelings.

Body movement is not the only vehicle for the expression of emotion. The voice and such paralinguistic features as pausing and speech rate, rhythm and intensity also provide evidence on emotional states. Moderate variations in pitch, for example, convey anger, boredom or disgust. Extreme variations convey surprise and happiness (La France and Mayo, 1978). Again it takes a skilled actor to control the voice in such a way as to either mask or project (falsify) a particular emotional state. What we do have is evidence that ordinary listeners can detect emotional states from the voice (Davitz and Davitz, 1959) and that they can detect deception from voice cues (Lavrakas and Maier, 1979).

Non-verbal communication as punctuation

The expression of emotion is only one of the functions of non-verbal communication. A second major function is that of illustrating and supporting speech. The management of a conversation is, as we have already seen, a complex and rule-governed affair, and body movement and gaze patterns show a synchrony which co-ordinates speech and listening. For written language we use punctuation to signal shifts in argument and topic; in speech and conversation we use non-verbal signals to help the listener to follow the content of what is being said. Of course, the listeners' task is that of providing speakers with feedback indicating that they are attending, understanding and responding either with agreement and approval or with disagreement or disapproval. They also have to indicate the wish to take the conversational floor, or to leave the encounter. Speakers' tasks are to plan the discourse so that listeners will understand, to monitor listeners' behaviour to see if in fact they are understanding, agreeing, etc., and to show them that they are handing the floor over to them. Language, fully occupied as it is with carrying the ideational content of the communication, could not carry all the information relating to the mechanics of social interaction as well, and it is non-verbal communication which is used for this purpose. Speech and non-verbal communication synchronize to an extent that has led at least one researcher to suggest that at some point they will have to be considered as inseparable, and that the task will be to uncover a grammar of all elements together, this domain being called 'etholinguistics' (Eibl-Eibesfeldt, in press). Let us return first to the listeners' behaviour.

Listeners look at speakers most of the time. They provide feedback in the form of empty linguistic markers like 'mm', 'yeah', but these are further emphasized by smiles, head nods and other movements, which are synchronized with them. Furthermore listeners maintain an expressive flow of facial expressions which echo the contents of speakers' discourse, that is frowns of commiseration, smiles of congratulation and shared pleasure, exaggerated astonishment, and so forth. At the point when listeners intend taking the floor their head nods become more rapid and their facial movements more exaggerated. These have been called 'turn claim' signals (Duncan, 1976), and this feedback is very important for speakers. It is extremely difficult and unnerving to talk to someone whose face remains completely immobile and impassive, but it is also irritating to have an acrobatic display of facial movements from listeners. The extent and nature of expressive feedback is limited by culturally specific rules. Mediterranean cultures permit a more dynamic level of expressiveness than, for example, Japanese or north Europeans.

The movements of the speaker punctuate the content of what is being said. For example the position of the whole trunk remains relatively constant while the topic is being maintained and a change of topic is marked by a gross shift in posture. Within a topic, shifts in the points being made are also mirrored by small head movements. These movements help the listener to understand the content of the speech and to prepare for shifts in topic (Scheflen, 1964).

Speakers look away as they start to speak and subsequently look only briefly at listeners in order to gather feedback from them. If the discourse is complex, in the sense that the material is unfamiliar or the ideas potentially 'tactless' or unpleasant for the listener, this will be shown up in slower, more hesitant speech, with longer pauses, both of the silent variety and of the 'filled' variety (filled with 'uuh', 'umm', etc.), and this less fluent speech will be accompanied by avoidance of looking at the listener (Kendon, 1970). Complex speech requires more 'planning' and therefore it is necessary to reduce the amount of information that is having to be processed. One source of distracting information is that emanating from the behaviour of listeners. Under normal circumstances speakers will glance only very briefly at the listeners to ensure that they are 'still there'. When they want to hand over the conversation to the listeners, they will signal this by falling intonation, relaxation of hand positions and most importantly a prolonged look. If the latter is not forthcoming or visible, turn-taking in conversation becomes a jerky affair, with long pauses between speakers and utterances or frequent interruptions (Duncan, 1976). Thus we can see that non-verbal signals are extremely important in the regulation of turn-taking and in the facilitation of comprehension and verbal planning.

Non-verbal communication and the establishment of dominance

A conversation is not, however, simply an exchange of information, or a passage of information from one party to another; it is one part of the process through which roles are formed and interpersonal relationships developed. This point is clear when we look at the establishment of dominance in conversations and when we look at synchrony and congruity. Let's take the case of dominance. A speaker can establish dominance in a conversation by establishing the topic, controlling switches in topic and keeping control over the conversational floor. One important strategy for maintaining dominance, once the topic has been established, is that of avoiding looking at the listener. In this way any feedback which might deflect from the conversational purpose can be avoided. Speakers will fail to see signs that listeners want to take the floor; they will be undeterred by signs of agreement, disagreement, approval, disapproval, boredom, embarrassment, failures of comprehension or anything else. Also they cannot mistakenly give the prolonged-glance signal that the listener might use as a turn-taking signal. Avoiding looking at other people when they are talking allows speakers to ignore the role of the glance in turn-taking. This allows them simply to talk down verbal attempts to take the floor. Ensuring that all pauses are 'filled' pauses also makes either turn-taking or interruption more difficult for the other person. In one study (La France and Carmen, 1980) it was found that dominant speakers looked at others less, smiled less, interrupted more and filled pauses. In that study the authors found that men with a high degree of stereotypically male characteristics showed this dominant conversational style. Looking in order to collect feedback is not the only kind of looking. Long gazes signal both interest and involvement in the other person, on the one hand, and threat, on the other. Which of these two contradictory states is inferred depends on other kinesic factors surrounding the gaze, for example facial expression. Kimble and Forte (1978) found that subjects asked to role-play 'involvement' in the message immediately looked at the speaker. The member of a group who is dominating the discussion characteristically uses a sweeping gaze across the whole group while talking, 'fixing' each of the group members briefly in turn. The stare is a threat signal amongst species other than man, and we have evidence that it operates similarly in man. For example, a prolonged stare from a stranger stimulates flight and avoidance. Teachers use the stare as a method of control in the classroom. For example, a prolonged gaze when something positive is being said enhances positive feeling, but a prolonged gaze while something negative is being said enhances negative feelings (Ellsworth and Carlsmith, 1968).

Accommodative behaviour

At the other end of the continuum from dominance and submission is accommodative behaviour – behaviour which enhances affiliation and mutual involvement. Looking as opposed to staring enables one to receive feedback from the other person and be influenced by it. Looking also signifies approval and openness, especially if it is accompanied by smiling. Head nods and expressive mimicry also serve to increase the congruency of the interaction. Congruency is also expressed in position. Two speakers who are in accord show this by shifting posture to match that of the other. If one leans forward, the other does so too. If one sits back in a relaxed way, so does the other (Scheflen, 1964). There is a considerable amount of research that suggests that people influence one another's expressive behaviour during interaction, that is that such features as pause lengths, vocal intensity, self-disclosure become more similar as the encounter proceeds (Cappella, 1980); moreover, failure to accommodate in this way may be a device for 'opting out' of the conversation, mutuality of behaviour appearing to be one component of harmonious encounters.

Proximity and touching also signal positive and intimate feelings. That is people take up a position closer to those they like and know well than they do to strangers. The actual size of the zone which people maintain around their persons depends on situational factors, but it also depends on culture. Arabs, and people from the Mediterranean generally, maintain closer proximity, touch more, engage in more eye contact and generally have a more 'intense' interactive style (Watson and Graves, 1966). We in the north often describe this style as 'warm', and they describe ours as 'cold' (Greeks maintain that interacting with north Europeans is like eating a dish of cold boiled rice without salt on it). But again we have to remember that non-verbal behaviours operate together and with verbal behaviour, both to reinforce and to compensate for each other. For example, when people disclose intimate information about themselves, often they will avert the gaze and turn the body away. Enforced close proximity may result in a reduction in eye contact (Argyle and Dean 1965). In parts of South America people have a typically Mediterranean style of interacting with much touching and close interpersonal distances. However, when it comes to terms of address they are considerably more formal in their use of titles and surnames than North Americans are. Yet the latter share the 'cold' modes of distance and non-touching of Northern Europe. Proximity, eye contact and touch taken together seem to reflect sex differences in style of interaction. For example women have a more 'immediate' and personal style to judge by the fact that they talk more, gesture more, gaze more, orient the body in more varied ways than men do (Ickes, 1978) and respond more positively to touch (Whitcher and Fisher, 1979). As far as touch is concerned, the latter study showed that one single touch by nursing staff in pre-operative female patients had significant and positive effects on their response to the surgery. The opposite was observed in men. It has been suggested (Henley, 1977) that higher-status people initiate touching of lower-status people and therefore for males it is a dominance signal rather than an affiliative one.

Culture – a source of mis-communication

One of the major problems in non-verbal communication is that of cultural specificity. With regard to non-verbal behaviour concerned with the expression of emotion, for example facial expression, we have evidence of great universality. However, for many other non-verbal elements, for example touching or the use of space in the regulation of social encounters, there is considerable cross-cultural variation.

When we learn to speak a foreign language we really need to learn the non-verbal components which orchestrate it. Italians, for example, orchestrate their speech with a wealth of gesture, including complex hand movements, shoulder shrugs and facial expressions. A spy trying to pass off as an Italian would have to have more than fluent Italian to do so without risk of detection. In our own society we interact with people of different ethnic and cultural origins, whose native language is some varient of standard English, who are assimilated in varying degrees to the dominant culture but whose non-verbal behaviour has subtle but important differences. These differences can lead to quite serious misunderstandings and misattribution of motives. For example it has been shown that the intonational patterns of Asians speaking English in Britain can lead to incorrect judgements of aggressiveness (Gumpertz *et al.*, 1979). Then, in one series of studies of the listening styles of blacks and whites in the United States, it was found that blacks give very subtle and minimal cues that they are listening, except at certain points in the interaction. These points, called 'listening response-relevant moments', are instants when a special listening response is required, for example at an emphatic comment from the speaker. At these moments, black people demonstrate a lot of kinesic activity. White people, however, provide much more vivid evidence of background listening, but less marked behaviour at the response-relevant moment. One of the major consequences of this is that white people often think that black people are not actually listening or attending at all. Clearly in contexts like educational ones, such misattribution could lead to judgements which would be damaging (Erickson, 1979).

It was the discovery of the hidden and largely inadvertent dimension of non-verbal communication that provided the most important stimulus towards considering social interaction as a form of skilled performance, and to thinking of unsatisfactory social behaviour as produced more by failures of skill than by more enduring emotional or motivational problems. Its largely inadvertent qualities also sensitized psychologists working in the field to the fact that feedback about such ignored or unattended-to aspects of behaviour could be richly revealing to clients and practitioners alike. In the later sections of this book we shall see some examples of such revelation.

6

Understanding other people –
the lay person's psychology

The professional psychologist's knowledge about psychological processes is an amalgam of theory and data. And so is that of the lay person.

Our knowledge about other people, their motives and characters, is the result of a trade-off between what we know, or think that we know, about them already, and data in the form of actual characteristics and actual behaviour and the contexts in which these are manifested. The process is similar to that involved in understanding language, both written and spoken. We rarely process every detail of the actual words that are spoken; instead we focus on what is meant or intended. Similarly, when we read off a printed page, we don't respond to every element of every letter, or even every word. We scan whole sentences and passages for the meaning, which we can so often guess at, from our existing knowledge, both non-linguistic and linguistic. The trade-off is such that the more that is already known the less information is required from the actual stimulus.

This process is central to the understanding of person perception. When we form impressions of others we are making guesses or inferences based both on whatever selection of data, derived from our observations of them, are at hand and the theories that we already have about them. The study of person perception is the study of how the lay person uses theory and data in understanding other people. As professionals we are going to spy on that process, psychologists studying the psychological theories and research of their lay psychologist colleagues.

Understanding other people's motives and characters is one of the central tasks which professionals and ordinary people have in common. Let us remind ourselves of some of the arguments put forward in chapter 1 about how the two parties differ in their approach to that task.

Person perception – the lay person versus the professional

First, as lay persons we use our theories for pragmatic and immediate purposes, rather than for the purpose of gaining knowledge for its own sake. For example we may have to decide rapidly whether someone is momentarily in a bad mood, as opposed to continually and chronically hostile, before we agree to share a flat with them. It is rare that lay persons sit back and attempt to assess the absolute truth of their beliefs and judgements. However, even when they do engage in such endeavours they are unlikely to be as strict as the professionals about assessing the data on which their judgements are based. Mostly they do not know whether the behaviour of their target person is a typical sample of the latter's behaviour or not. Mostly the data they have is simply that which happens to be currently available, and which happens to have caught their attention: now they focus on appearance; tomorrow on behaviour with the family; the day after on something someone else has said about them. They may never explicitly relate those three types of data to each other. Not only that; they may fail to remember or even notice data which are incongruent with what is already 'known', and attend simply to those which are congruent with existing beliefs. For example, we may know someone who is French. Everyone 'knows' that French people are great gourmets and excellent cooks. Our someone is actually quite uninterested in food and only occasionally cooks an elaborate meal. But it will be the occasional meal which we will notice and use as evidence for our someone's Frenchness, and not the much more frequent evidence of fast foods and hastily prepared snacks.

Then, unlike the professional scientist, we are rarely disinterested observers of other's behaviours. We may have many vested interests in forming particular impressions of others. We do not want to know the shortcomings of some person we have fallen in love with, or the unreliability of someone we have to depend on, or the formidable talents of a rival. Most of all we have a vested interest in the idea that other people are predictable and controllable, and, if possible, quite simple to understand. Of course the professionals have to watch themselves too in this respect; it can happen that a researcher, with a theory on which a professional reputation stands, finds supporting evidence for that theory which rivals do not find in their research. But therein lies the difference. The professional has to pass through a minefield of alternative views and researchers eager to put theories to the test. For lay persons it is quite rare for others to know directly what their implicit theories of others actually are.

So the task of the professional in this case is that of finding out how ordinary people form impressions of each other. In spite of all that has been said about the relative shortcomings of the lay person in relating theory and data, we are not here concerned primarily with the accuracy of the lay person's judgements, only in the processes by which they are formed. Indeed it is quite difficult to take up any other position, since knowledge of the ultimate truth about others is probably indeterminate. All that we can do is compare the judgements of individuals and the judgements of the majority about some person; or compare the judgements of the individual or individuals and 'objective' measures like personality tests; or compare the individual and the experienced clinician; or simply set a behavioural criterion with which the individual's predictions about another can be compared. Each of these sources has components of 'error' or bias which allow them to be only partial indices of the 'reality' of a person. For the most part we shall be concerned simply with the way in which certain types of information regularly appear to produce certain inferences and judgements. In the later sections of this book we shall be concerned with ways in which clients can be made more aware of their implicit theories of others, and be more critical of the information which is used to maintain a theory, because, of course, in the long run we want them to be aware of their implicit theories and the relationship between these theories and their actions and relationships with others.

The research literature on person perception *can* lead to the impression that ordinary people make detailed analyses of other people's motives and characters all the time. But of course this is neither true nor necessary. When psychologists (professionals, that is) do studies of person perception, they involve their subjects in the task of making quite extensive analyses of another's characteristics or motives. That is subjects make extensive judgements because they have been asked to, on the basis of information they have been given. What we must remember is that we do not really know how extensive people's spontaneous everyday judgements *customarily* are. After all, for much of the time our perceptions of others take place in contexts where our knowledge of a person's social role and the expectations associated with it suffices for us to be able to predict the other's behaviour, and therefore orient our conduct towards that person. Our interactions with bank clerks, nurses, policemen, and even with members of our own families, are dictated by well-established scenarios. For example we do not need to know anything about the *personality* of a bank clerk to be able to predict what he or she will do when we hand in a paying-in slip and some money. The discussion of social roles and situations in chapter 3 has already revealed how much behaviour is constrained by the rules pertaining to both. The lay psychologist knows this too, and understanding the rules of roles and situations may suffice for many practical purposes.

Then, lay persons may not make an extensive analysis of another's character because they have assigned the person to some category, for example a racial or physical category for which they have a ready stereotype, which they feel suffices for everyday purposes. Stereotypes are beliefs about the characteristics possessed by some group and possessed therefore by any member of that group. For example, there is a widespread belief that physically attractive people are happier, nicer and more competent than are physically unattractive people (Berscheid and Walster, 1974). Then, there is, of course, a voluminous research literature on stereotypes of different ethnic groups. In one study subjects were shown photographs of fifteen girls projected on to a screen and asked to rate them for beauty, ambition, intelligence, character, etc. Two months later the procedure was repeated with the following additions: fifteen new pictures were added in order to distract subjects from the real nature of the experiment and fictitious names were given to the girls in such a way that some of the thirty girls had obviously Jewish names, others Irish, others Italian, others Anglo-Saxon. The greatest deterioration in rating was shown in the ratings for likability and character of the 'Jewish' photographs, in which, similarly, the greatest improvement in ratings was shown for intelligence and ambition (Razran, 1950).

The professional research literature concerned with person perception divides into two major areas of study. One is concerned with how ordinary people assess the causes and reasons behind other people's behaviour. This area of research is called 'attribution theory'. The other is concerned with the impressions we form of other people's characters. In both areas we are interested in the trade-off process, that is the knowledge and theories others bring to bear on their judgements, as well as their use of information deriving from the person being judged.

Attribution processes

We are indebted to Fritz Heider for stimulating interest in the lay person's understanding of causes in behaviour. In his book *The Psychology of Interpersonal Relations*, he explored the ways in which lay persons make causal analyses of the behaviour of others, of the ways in which they understand relationships, and so forth (Heider, 1958).

When we make inferences or predictions about others, the basic data available are usually their behaviour and the context in which it occurs. We can only use that behaviour as a basis for prediction and inference if we know what caused it. For example an angry, insulting remark from someone takes on a completely different significance if we know that it is the end point of a situation where that person has been unmercifully provoked, rather than a response to a mild query. In the first case we locate a fair amount of the cause in the situation; in the second case we locate the cause in the individual's mood or even disposition. It is only in the second case that we have a basis for forming confidently an impression of that person. To use behaviour as a basis for impression formation, then, we have to decide the extent to which it is produced by external forces or internal forces.

External forces are many. They can be factors in the physical environment, like temperature, noise, isolation, overcrowding and barriers of all sorts. External forces can be the expectations associated with particular situations, that is the rules of situations. For example, we do not judge people's usual mood from their behaviour at a funeral, or for that matter from their behaviour at a hectic party. Similarly, external forces can derive from the demands associated with particular social roles. For example, it can be quite difficult to judge the personality of a hospital matron simply from observing her at work. External forces can also be such things as luck or chance, if we believe in them, or the action of the gods, if we believe in them.

Internal or personal forces are located within the mind of the person being judged: moods, abilities, motives and goals, enduring dispositional qualities like generosity or cunning, liabilities like strong habits or addictions, fears and obsessions. Situations may not recur, the physical environment may change, roles are limited to particular times and places; behaviour which is caused, or at least strongly influenced, by such factors also may never occur again and therefore as causes they provide little basis for prediction. But *internal* factors are carried around by the individual, and it is *internal* causes which provide us with a firmer basis for making judgements and predictions about others, and which we prefer. After Heider's initial essays on the lay psychologist's attribution of causes to internal and external factors, attribution theory was taken up by a number of other psychologists, among them Harold Kelley (1967).

Kelley suggested that lay observers set about the task of attributing causes of behaviour in an extremely systematic fashion, rather like their professional colleagues do. He suggested that observers look for co-variation between possible causes and behaviours, so that they look for conditions present when a behaviour occurs and conditions absent when the behaviour does not occur. Thus if Hilda always wears a green frock when Harry comes to dinner, and never wears it otherwise, then the observer locates the cause of her choice of dress in Harry's anticipated presence. In making this analysis, observers take into account three types of information: first they ask themselves whether the

84

behaviour occurs in any situations other than the one just observed. For example a man runs away from a barking dog. Does he always behave in a fearful way with all dogs, or only this one? This information relates to the distinctiveness of the behaviour in the particular situation. Then they ask themselves whether he behaves in the same way on every occasion, or only on this one. This information relates to the consistency of the behaviour over time. Finally they ask themselves about the extent to which other people behave similarly when confronted with this dog. This is called consensus information. If the actor behaves similarly across varying situations (low distinctiveness), behaves similarly on different occasions (high consistency), and others do not behave the same way as the actor does (low consensus), then the observer assumes that the cause of the behaviour lies within the actor rather than within the situation. Conversely, high distinctiveness, low consistency and high consensus would lead the observer to assume that the situation was responsible for the behaviour.

Kelley's model was sufficiently precisely formulated to be put easily to the empirical test. A number of researchers did so. Their basic technique involved presenting subjects with information about an imaginary person's actions and information relating to distinctiveness, consistency and consensus in such a way that different groups of subjects had information showing each of the three factors to be high, medium or low in every combination possible (McArthur, 1972). Of the three types of information consistency and distinctiveness had the most effect on subjects' judgements. High consistency and low distinctiveness led to internal attributions. Consensus information, however, had far less effect, that is information that others had or had not acted in the same way in those circumstances had less bearing on judging the cause of the action to be within the actor.

How might we explain this? It could have been to do with the fact that information about how others have acted tells us no more at all about the actor, and it is information about the actor that we need. But other researchers have considered consensus information from a slightly different viewpoint. Jones and Davis (1965), in their work on correspondent inferences (a correspondent inference is one where the link between a behaviour and a disposition is direct) have suggested that the normativeness or social desirability of an action lessens our confidence in attributing it to internal causes. For example if someone puts forward an unpopular opinion to an unsympathetic audience, one judges that opinion to be a sincere reflection of the speaker's true views. If someone puts forward a viewpoint that everyone present thoroughly approves of – then we are not so sure it represents true opinions. Thus Jones and Davis are suggesting that it is what we *imagine* most people would do in the circumstances which provides the real consensus information rather than what other people *actually* do. Thus we assume that most people will bow to social pressures, and if the actor does not, then this provides us with a basis for inferring an internal cause.

One of the problems of the McArthur study and of Kelley's model is that it is based on very unusual situations. Very often people do not have information which relates to distinctiveness, consistency or consensus at all. It is *they* who have to collect that information. The questions are then: Do they bother to collect it? and: Do they collect it systematically? Kelley of course was aware that such information was often not available, and he argued that in these situations people relied on 'causal schemata', that is, on the one hand, some kind of theory about what the three sources of information would be, if only one could get hold of them, and, on the other hand, preferences for certain types of cause. The work of Nisbett and Ross (1980) has shown that one of the most usual errors made is to assume behaviour to be more representative of the actor's repertoire than it actually is and so under-estimate distinctiveness and over-estimate consistency when information is lacking (or sometimes even when it isn't!).

One aspect of causal schemata, on which we have evidence, is that of relating extreme effects to extreme causes. For example if someone does something dramatic, like suddenly packing up their things and emigrating to the other side of the world, we usually attribute this to a 'strong' cause, like being in trouble with the law, or severe disappointment in love, rather than the actor having just picked up a travel brochure about the pleasures of Australia. When Kennedy was killed there was a strong move towards attributing his assassination (strong effect) to a complex plot (strong cause) rather than the action of one unimportant individual (weak cause).

Another aspect of causal schemata is our expectations about a particular actor's behaviour. For example if an actor behaves in a way which in our schemata is unexpected or unusual, we are motivated both to look for causes in the first place, as well as to show a preference for internal causes (Jones and McGillis, 1976). Expectations which provide input to causal schemata are of two sorts. One derives from our expectations about the group of which the actor is a member. For example someone may have expectations about the poor academic performance of black school children. The brilliant performance of a black school child will thus be surprising and start the observer scanning the individual characteristics of that child to locate the cause internally in its intelligence, rather than, for example, in the relatively low demands of the academic tasks to which it is put. The other derives from our expectations of an individual based on past experience (really a form of consistency information, though not necessarily tied to a particular situation). The decision of a comfort-loving, materialistic friend to sell off his or her worldly goods would alert our attention to the need to scan once again the friend's personality for evidence of propensities which could account for this behaviour. Lalljee *et al*. (1982) found that explanations of unexpected behaviour were more complex than for expected behaviour. If the situation was familiar and the behaviour unexpected, the explanation was in terms of person elements. If the situation was unfamiliar and behaviour unfamiliar it was explained by situation elements.

It is highly likely that people do resort to causal schemata which represent their beliefs that certain types of cause are inherently more probable than others, regardless of the actual information available. But the problem for the attribution theorist remains that of finding how people collect information relevant to making causal analyses in the first place. There is evidence that their sampling of relevant information is in fact quite biased. A number of studies have shown that the perceptual salience or vividness of information claims our attention and biases the attribution process. In one study (Taylor *et al*., 1979) the researchers manipulated the salience of an actor by manipulating the uniqueness of his race. Subjects observed a discussion between six males. Some saw groups composed of 5 white men and 1 black while others saw groups composed of 3 black and 3 white. They found, for example, that the influence of a black actor on the group was seen as far stronger when he was alone among white men than when the same actor was viewed (doing exactly the same things) with a mixed group. Similar findings emerged from studies where salience was varied via the sex composition of groups, and even here actors were made salient by being surrounded by additional illumination (McArthur and Post, 1977).

Then the *effects* of an action can make it salient and initiate a search for the cause. For example if an action results in a severe outcome (particularly if it is severe for the observer, such as someone buckling the door of a new car in circumstances the owner knows nothing about), there is a tendency for more responsibility to be located within the actor than in the circumstances (Harvey *et al.* 1975).

Whether we are considering an observer's use of information which has been provided, or whether we are concerned with the processes by which an observer selects information in making causal judgements, there is a strong tendency for observers to prefer internal causes and to seek information justifying internal causes. We tend to under-estimate or even ignore situational influences on behaviour. A study by Ross illustrates the process well (Ross *et al.*, 1977). Subjects were recruited for a game involving tests of general knowledge. Subjects were either participants or observers and all saw that the former were randomly allocated to the roles of questioners or contestants. The questioners were told that they were to ask the contestants any general-knowledge question they cared to choose out of their own stock of general knowledge, the proviso being, of course, that they should know the answers. The contestants were to answer as best they could. After the game had finished, observers, contestants and questioners alike were asked to rate contestants and questioners on their general knowledge and other competence-related questions. In spite of the strong situational factors which allowed the questioners to display their knowledge and gave little opportunity for the contestants to display theirs, the latter received lower ratings by all parties, even themselves.

Why should we be reluctant to attribute people's actions to situational factors? There are a number of reasons. First (as has been mentioned before) internal causes make people's behaviour appear more predictable as they provide a basis for further inference. Predictability enhances one's sense of control over the environment which, as we shall see in chapter 7, is important for people's sense of well-being. Secondly, for us as observers the actor is usually more salient than the situation, that is the actor claims more of our attention, thus directing our search for causal factors within him or her, simply because we are more aware of the actor than the situation. Also even if we are aware of features in the current situation, we seldom know what has led up to the situation, so that often it is difficult to interpret.

The consequences of attributing the causes of behaviour to the actor's intentions and dispositions, and thus from these attributions to further inferences about the person's characteristics, can have profound effects on our relationships with that person. One feature of social-skills training must involve an analysis of clients' beliefs about the causes of the behaviour of those with whom they regularly interact. Let us now turn to examine the other process of forming impressions of others.

Forming impressions of other people's characters

Our impressions of others and the implicit predictions we make about them are produced partly by our observations of them, and other available information about them, and partly by our theories of how personality is organized and structured. For example we might have a theory that a person whom we know to be extremely tidy and obsessional in habits will also be punctilious about keeping time, very careful with money and prone to give a lot of thought to decisions before acting, even though we do not have any data on these last three tendencies. Such a theory is an implicit theory of personality. Let us start by looking at the various ways in which implicit theories of personality have been studied.

In one technique subjects are told that person X has the attribute y. They are then asked to rate the likelihood that X will have other attributes a, b and c. From a number of subjects it is possible to see the extent to which attributes co-occur and, given any one, to predict the extent of association between it and any other. The limitation of such a method, called the trait-inference method, lies in the fact that the investigator chooses the trait words, which might not have been the ones which the subjects would have spontaneously used. Furthermore it is not clear whether one is really studying people's beliefs about the co-variation of real traits in people, or simply the closeness in meaning of sets of words applied to personality. For example it may be that people rate as high the likelihood that a slow person will also be deliberate. This might not in fact refer to a belief about the usual coincidence of these two qualities in people, but simply to the belief that 'slow' and 'deliberate' have almost the same meanings, whether applied to people or not.

Another technique involves subjects rating people they actually know on a number of personality traits. If the traits intelligent, tidy, energetic always get the same level of rating then this is evidence that they co-occur, at least in the minds of the subjects. The researcher would calculate the correlation coefficient (a statistical estimate of the degree of association between two variables) between each trait and every other trait, and this would be the basis for representing an implicit theory of personality. This method does allow the subjects to apply traits to their knowledge of actual people; however, they are still having to use traits which may not be the ones that they would use spontaneously. Probably then, the most satisfactory evidence on the extent and nature of people's implicit theories of personality will be derived from their spontaneous descriptions, although even here there are two levels of spontaneity. For example, at one level one can ask subjects to describe one or more people that they know using any terms that they wish. However, it still just may be that they never spontaneously summarize the personalities of people that they know. The other level of spontaneity is even better. This is where people have written or talked about others without realizing that their descriptions would be studies at all. One famous example of such an approach to the study of an individual's implicit personality theory is that concerned with the American novelist Theodore Dreiser (Rosenberg and Jones, 1972). In one of his novels, *A Gallery of Women*, he describes a large number of fictional characters, which one can treat as free description (since the characters only exist in the author's head it is a particularly acute way of examining his implicit personality theory). Rosenberg and Jones listed all the words and terms used in descriptions and then computed the number of times each co-occurred in a description of the same character. The degree of association between traits was then examined by using the multi-dimensional scaling technique described in chapter 3 (recall that in that instance the data were the number of times observers placed social situations in the same category). The authors found that two dimensions lay behind the theory of Theodore Dreiser. One was the sex of the character. In his implicit personality theory, males and females had different characters. The other was their degree of conformity. In his mind he entertained two types, one successful and conforming, the other free and unconventional. Thus, for him, the two main features which differentiate people were whether they were male or female and whether they were conventional or not.

Finally another powerful method of uncovering people's theories of personality is that adopted by George Kelly (Kelly, 1955) and called the 'repertory grid technique'. This technique involves asking subjects to write down the names of people who occupy particular roles, like mother, boss, best friend, colleague, most disliked person. Each role is paired with two others in every possible combination, and the subjects are asked to say in what way two of them are alike and unlike the third. In this way a list of the 'constructs' which the subject uses in thinking about people is obtained. With this basic information it is also possible to find out what the dimensions of the constructs are, by asking the subjects to supply the opposites of the terms they have listed; to examine the linkages between the constructs, by asking them if one construct within a person were to change what other constructs would also change; and so forth. The use of the technique was primarily clinical at first, but it can be seen as a powerful instrument for uncovering people's implicit theories of personality.

Having looked at some techniques which professional psychologists have developed for studying the theories of their lay colleagues, let us look now at research which examines the influence of these theories in processing information about others.

We do not attend to all the information which is available to us about other characters. The importance of vividness and salience have already been alluded to in the discussion of attributing causes. In addition there is the factor of relevance and usefulness. Much of the information we process about others is relevant to some task that we have immediately to hand. For example, in making inferences about someone with whom we are going on a highly dangerous mountaineering expedition, information relating to the person's emotionality or potential response to danger and discomfort is more likely to be processed than information about his or her originality.

It is our existing schemata or theories which have major effects on our utilization of information at all stages of the process. We have already discussed implicit theories of personality structure. These also take the form of stereotypes or expectations about different categories or groups of people, people who are linked in the mind of the observer because they have the same racial characteristics, or because they are physically attractive, or even because they wear glasses or play bowls. Take for example the following experiment. Subjects were shown a video of a discussion between two males. They were told that they were actually watching a 'live' interaction over closed-circuit television. While they were watching the interaction they were instructed to classify a piece of behaviour, for example 'agrees' or 'disagrees', whenever they were given a signal by the experimenter. At one point the discussion becomes heated and one actor gives the other a shove. Then the screen goes blank. The interest lies in how the subjects classify the shove. In fact the subjects have been divided into different groups which each see a version of the same film which differs only in the race of the two actors. The scheme is represented below:

Protagonist	Victim
white	white
white	black
black	white
black	black

The categories that the subjects had available for classifying the shove were as follows: 'playing around'; dramatizing; aggressive behaviour; violent behaviour. Many more subjects classified the black protagonists' behaviour as violent than so classified the whites' behaviour, particularly if the victim was white. Thus the subjects' expectations of schemata for blacks and whites strongly influenced the way they interpreted identical behaviour (Duncan, 1976).

Just as we are selective in our attention to and classification or interpretation of behaviour, so our theories and schemata influence also our *recall* of information about others.

In one study subjects were read an account of some events in the life of a woman. Sometime later they were given some additional information. Some of them were told that the woman had met a lesbian and had started a homosexual relationship with her. Others were told that she had met a man and started a heterosexual relationship with him. The remainder were given no information regarding the woman's sexual relationships. A week later they were all given a test to see if they could recall details of her earlier life, for example, whether or not she had dated boys in her early adolescence. The first group showed strong distortion effects in the way they recalled events in the woman's earlier life, the distortions being in line with stereotypes about the typical characters of lesbians.

Furthermore we may reclassify past information about an individual on the basis of some present designation. For example when people have psychological breakdowns and become psychotic or unmanageable in some way, their closest kin often rewrite their biographies, or rather the meanings of their biographies, in the light of the newly available interpretation of them. Behaviour previously accepted as normal or positive may be thought now as having been an indicator of their 'real' characters. For example: 'I always thought Joan's quietness/sociability/sensitivity/insensitivity was a bit odd – now I can see what it was leading up to.' The assessment of a person's character then becomes retrospective.

Although our implicit theories of personality could be considered in many dimensions, one of the most important is that of evaluation. We are not indifferent to traits and certainly prefer some to others. Our impressions of others are easily described in terms of an evaluative, or like-versus-dislike dimension. This is very apparent when we consider the effects of order on impression formation. Many different studies have found evidence for the priority of *first* impressions over later impressions in terms of overall favourability. This effect holds unless subjects are specifically instructed to attend closely to all information (Hendrick and Constanini, 1970). What is of most practical interest, however, is that a negative first impression is more resistant to change than a positive one is (Hodges, 1974). One reason for this is likely to be that negative information carries more weight than positive because it is likely to reflect socially undesirable traits or behaviours and therefore the observer can be more confident in attributing the behaviour or trait to the person's 'real' nature (recall the work of Jones and Davis (1965), described in the previous section, on the role of normativeness on correspondent inferences). The other possible reason could be that it is more adaptive for us to beware of negative traits than it is to approach positive ones. That is we need to know more about people's potentially negative effects than about their potential benefits.

The self-fulfilling prophecy

If the impressions we make of others remained as impressions, inside our heads, as those of academic psychologists often stay inside journals and books, their power would be quite limited. However they do not stay there. Usually they insinuate themselves into behaviour with concomitant effects on others. Our impressions of others, derived from whatever source, can create self-fulfilling prophecies. That is by translating our beliefs about others into behaviour we may make those beliefs more true.

In one study (Snyder et al., 1977) male subjects were asked to speak for a few minutes over the phone to an unknown female. The purpose behind this research was, supposedly, to study the acquaintance process. The males were assigned to one of two experimental groups. In one group they were told that the woman was very attractive; in the other group they were told that she was very unattractive. Then the men were asked to rate the woman (having spoken to her) on other traits. The telephone conversation was recorded in such a way that observers could either hear just the man's contributions or just the woman's contributions. The observers knew nothing about the attractiveness manipulation. The observers were then asked to rate the woman on the basis of what they had heard of the conversation, and similarly the man. The findings were highly revealing of the effects of self-fulfilling prophecies.

The males' ratings of their telephone partners showed clear effects of the attractiveness manipulation, with the 'physically attractive' woman being judged more positively than the 'physically unattractive' woman on traits which had nothing to do with physical attractiveness. The observers' ratings of the woman they heard on the telephone (remember that they know nothing about either her appearance or, more importantly, about the male partner's *beliefs* about her appearance) showed a clear bias. The 'attractive' one was judged as more confident; more animated; enjoying the conversation; liking the partner. The 'physically unattractive' woman was rated as more sensitive; altruistic; kind; genuine; modest. Their ratings suggested that the men actually behaved differently under the two conditions. The men in the 'physically attractive' group were rated as: more sociable; sexually warm; interesting; independent; permissive; bold; outgoing; humorous; socially adept; enjoying the encounter more, and so on.

The serious consequences of the processes of self-fulfilling prophecy are well illustrated in contexts where peoples' judgements of one another really matter. In the worlds of psychiatric clinics, school classrooms and reformatories, for example, life careers are at risk. Let us look at some studies conducted in these real-life contexts.

Denzin (1968) asked a number of psychiatrists to fill in a questionnaire about each new patient admitted to a state mental hospital during a specified period. A few weeks later they were asked how many personal-therapy sessions the patients had received. In the initial questionnaires they were asked about their perceptions of the patients' attitudes towards psychiatric treatment and hospitals and their prognosis of the patients' recovery. Denzin hypothesized that the more favourable a patient's attitude towards the psychiatric line, the more favourable the prognosis, the more therapy the patient would get and the sooner he or she would leave hospital, all of which were confirmed by Denzin's data. Thus the patients' attitudes (as opposed to their psychiatric conditions) set up expectations on the part of the therapists about their conditions, and the influence of these expectations changed the therapists' behaviour towards the patients, which in turn brought about exactly what they had (implicitly) been predicting.

Meichenbaum *et al.*, (1969) selected 6 girls out of a class of 14 adolescents in a school for juvenile offenders, and told their teachers that they had high academic potential and were 'late bloomers'. Observers' ratings showed subsequent differences in the behaviour of the teachers towards those girls, and on later objective examinations the group (who of course had been matched with the others on actual academic potential, classroom behaviour and amount of attention normally received from the teachers) performed significantly better.

Particularly when we are talking about stigmatized individuals like the mentally ill or the criminally deviant, the expectations set up by the initial commitment procedures and the impressions of character formed by such procedures make a stigmatized career almost irreversible in many cases. The research literature on the self-fulfilling nature of expectations is now so voluminous that, as two erstwhile sceptics put it, 'the question for future research is not whether there are expectancy effects, but how they operate' (Baker and Crist, 1971).

Can we know others?

Lay persons show, in the processes of thinking and making inferences about one another, departures from the criteria established by scientific logic for such processes (Nisbett and Ross, 1980). But it is particularly difficult to know the extent to which they are actually wrong in their *conclusions*. That is they may arrive at the correct destination by tortuous routes filled with blind alleys, but we don't really know if they are right. Let us remind ourselves of the criteria that might be used for judging the accuracy of the lay person's judgements about others: comparisons of the judgements of different groups differing in their familiarity with the target person; comparisons with standardized tests assessing the target person; comparison with the target person's self-judgement. In fact none of these criteria may in themselves be more veridical than any other because they may in fact be based on different perspectives and different available information. In the next chapter we shall be exploring the processes by which people make inferences about themselves, and this will reveal that even these judgements can be subject to the same processes and the same problems of establishing validity.

These arguments led earlier to the proposition that knowledge of others is essentially indeterminant. There are, however, additional arguments for this proposition. Take, for example, the question of the reasons given for people's behaviour. Very often when we give reasons for behaviour it is in response to the demands of the moment, that is to what we believe the listener needs to know. The question 'Why did Lucy marry Harry?' may require rather different answers according to whether the underlying question is one of the following:

Why did Lucy marry Harry [rather than anyone else]?
Why did Lucy marry Harry [rather than just live with him]?
Why did Lucy marry Harry [rather than stay single]?
Why would anyone marry Harry?
What was it about *Harry* that made Lucy marry him [one of the 'attribution-theory' questions]?
What was it about *Lucy* that made her marry Harry [another 'attribution-theory' question]?
What were the factors in Lucy's childhood that made her . . . [asked in the context of a conversation on psychoanalytic themes]?
What are the factors in Lucy's life situation that are leading her towards . . . [asked in the context of a feminist discussion]?

All these and many more suggest that myriad answers are available because there are myriad questions. The answers can be judged more in terms of their social aptness than in terms of their correctness.

What another's character is 'really' like may not be a reasonable question, because the only reality is the perceiver's perception. Show a video of a patient speaking about his life and problems and ask a psychoanalyst, a behavourist, a sociologist and a medical doctor what they see and hear, and not only will they each report different things but it is possible that they will all be 'right' from the point of view of their own perspectives.

Then, the presence of self-fulfilling prophecies also undermines our belief in the determinancy of knowledge. If it is true that when we interact with other people our impressions, our actual acts of perception, *create* the reality of the other person, then there could be no reality beyond that which we are creating and therefore no firm criterion for correctness of judgement.

To strike a less gloomy note let us see what is positive about our perceptions of others and the uses to which they are put. One of the features of lay psychologists' judgements which bring great advantage to them, but great difficulty to the professional psychologists who are studying them, is their potentially malleable nature. For example, we may form a very favourable first impression of someone who is beautiful because of the stereotype we hold about the relationship between desirable psychological characteristics and desirable physical characteristics. But we don't have to stay with that impression. We can modify it in the light of further information. We may only notice further information which fits the already formed impression, but if we instruct ourselves actually to look for information which is incongruent with our impression, of course we can do so.

Nearly all the research discussed in this chapter has been based on people making judgements immediately on the basis of the limited information available. But in real life we don't need to make judgements very often, very explicitly or immediately. What we may need to learn to do is to distinguish carefully between situations where a judgement of someone is needed and situations where it is not and where it would be quite premature to make one and much better to keep an 'open mind'. When we make premature judgements, or fail to make judgements when for practical reasons we should, or are insufficiently aware of the fact that implicit judgements of others are informing our behaviour, we can modify all these judgements. Perception is a dynamic rather than a static process, and it is that feature which can be capitalized on by those wanting to change themselves and their relationships with other people.

7

Knowledge and experience of self

The most consistent thread running through our daily experience, whether we are with other people or not, is that of self-awareness, and that awareness is multi-faceted.

First, we are aware of events inside ourselves which are not accessible to other people. They are bodily, in the form of sensations, and psychological in the form of thoughts and images and memories. These are accessible to other people to the extent that we are able and willing to communicate them.

Secondly, we are aware of the public aspects of ourselves, how we appear to other people as physical objects (or, more precisely, how we think we appear to other people), and how we imagine we appear to others as characters.

Thirdly, we believe, with varying degrees of conviction, that we are the agents of our own actions, that we make our own decisions, that we choose to act this way or that, that we make goals for ourselves and direct ourselves towards them – that is we attribute the causes of our action to factors within ourselves. This belief varies between people and at different times in the same person.

For example we may speak about not being able to stop smoking, or eating, or 'getting involved in' courses of action which we don't really want to 'get involved in'. Colouring all this awareness is that of self-esteem or the general value that we place upon ourselves.

Mostly it is only people whom the rest of us would regard as quite abnormal who talk about being controlled by mysterious forces like radio waves. Although many of us at times play with the idea of our lives being controlled by astrological forces, or other devices of fate, these ideas tend to have a degree of curiosity value about them which underlines the more general feeling that we *are* in fact *agents* of what happens to us.

Oddly enough, there is a contrast here between what we as ordinary people *generally* believe, that is that we control our own behaviour, and many of the ideas that have evolved from those of professional psychologists. The latter, particularly if they are behaviourists, prefer to think of human action as controlled by stimuli from the environment, which ultimately will be measurable in their effects, or by physiological events which will turn out to be similarly measurable. With a complete understanding of these causative forces the psychologist should be able to predict behaviour and control it, and the concept of 'self as agent' would find no place in psychology. Naturally we do not classify psychologists as either lunatics or eccentrics in believing behaviour to be controlled by factors other than self, but that way of thinking seems not to accord well with what we normally experience. The question of whether our behaviour is determined in the way that they suggest, or whether we exercise free will, which is what we usually feel, is an issue which cannot occupy space here. As we shall see shortly, psychologists have neatly side-stepped the general philosophical issue and occupied themselves instead with the widespread belief that we do control our own affairs, and with the effects on behaviour and experience of assaults of that belief.

We have described several forms of self-awareness: awareness of private physical and psychological events; awareness of ourselves as public objects and characters; awareness of our value; awareness of ourselves as controllers of our own actions. Each of these has relevance for how we act and interact with others.

Although we are self-conscious or self-aware a lot of the time, we are not so all the time. The distinction has been continually drawn between two states of consciousness. One is that of subjective self-awareness, a state in which we are so absorbed in some activity that the only form of self-awareness is that deriving from the sensations of doing the task. Quickly trying to solve an algebraic equation, or threading a needle, or running to catch the last bus are so absorbing that we are not aware of ourselves as objects at all. The other state is that of objective self-awareness where we have space in our consciousnesses to be aware of ourselves as objects in our own eyes and in the eyes of other people (Wicklund, 1975). (It is important not to confuse this meaning of the term 'objective', that is the sense of oneself as an object, with its more usual meaning of 'absence of subjective bias'.) Imagine for example being very absorbed in a game of tennis which is requiring total concentration (*subjective* self-awareness) and then noticing that there is quite a little crowd watching the game. It is quite likely that one's attention would switch to an awareness of how one appeared to the audience and indeed to oneself (*objective* self-awareness). Wicklund argued that the two types of awareness cannot exist at the same moment in anyone's mind, but only fluctuate, possibly quite rapidly, between the two. He also argued that objective self-awareness was for the most part disagreeable, because our standards of how we would like to be are nearly always somewhat ahead of how we *actually* appear to ourselves. Objective self-awareness, whether it is induced by the presence of spectators, a sudden glimpse of oneself in a mirror, hearing oneself on a tape-recording, or whatever, is usually quite a nasty little shock. The only times when it is not are those when we have just experienced an astounding success, are dressed-up and looking our best, have been awarded a prize, have pulled off a successful performance, those few moments before our aspirations for ourselves catch up and overtake the reality.

Some researchers have argued that people vary in the level at which they habitually attend to the self. Some people are preoccupied with their own thoughts and feelings, bodily sensations and how they appear to others – that is they are usually objectively self-aware. Others have their attention directed away from the self most of the time. Fenigstein *et al*. (1975) developed a questionnaire for assessing this *chronic* level of self-awareness. They found there were three discriminable aspects to it. One was to do with people's attention to private thoughts, motives and feelings; another was concerned with how people appear to other people;

the third was concerned with the degree of social anxiety and discomfort people feel about their public performances.

In this chapter, particular aspects of self-awareness have been selected for special attention: broadly, awareness of oneself as agent, and perception and evaluation of oneself as a character. Finally we shall look briefly at the importance of self-disclosure, that is the willingness to make public private self-experience.

Awareness of self as agent

In order to act effectively people need to sustain a sense of control over their environment and to believe that they have some control over what happens to them. Again we are not concerned with the ultimate issues of whether people 'really' control their environment, their outcomes or indeed their own behaviour, but simply with their belief that they do so. There have been a number of research projects concerned with the belief itself; with the effects of clearly uncontrollable events on behaviour; with the effects of limiting people's freedom to act as they will; with the degree to which individuals vary in their belief that they do control their own outcomes.

Let us look at evidence for the belief itself. In a series of experiments, Langer (1975) showed how people generally over-estimate the degree of control that they have over events. For example in one study people were offered lottery tickets. In one group they were allowed to choose their own numbers; in the other group they were allocated them. Since the winning number was selected absolutely randomly there was no way in which the individual's act of choice could affect the probability of winning, and the probability was in fact identical for both groups. However, the subjects who chose their numbers apparently believed that they had a better chance of winning, since when asked how much money they would want for re-selling their tickets they consistently asked for higher prices than the other group did.

But what happens when people are *given* clear evidence that there is no relationship between their actions and what happens to them? Suppose, for example, we put subjects in an experimental situation in which they are going to receive electric shocks, which are unpleasant, but in which one group has control over when the shocks occur while the other group does not; or one group has an escape button which they may use if they want, and the other group has no such control; or one group may modify the shock by solving certain puzzles correctly and the other group may not. What effects might these manipulations have on them? In some early work with animals, Seligman and his associates (1975) found that exposure to uncontrollable negative outcomes of this sort resulted eventually in complete passivity on the part of the animals so that they no longer tried to escape, a response which came to be known as 'learned helplessness'. This was thought to be similar to the behaviour of severely depressed humans.

In one study (Geer *et al.*, 1970), forty subjects were given mild electric shocks through electrodes attached to their ankles and were instructed to press a reaction-time key as soon as they felt the shock. The shock lasted for six seconds on each trial, however quickly the subjects pressed the key. Half the subjects were then told that if their reaction time was speeded up they could reduce duration of shock by 50 per cent. The other half were told simply that there would be a reduction. On two measures of stress arousal those in the first (controllable-duration) condition showed diminishing stress. However, experimental studies in a laboratory setting with human subjects have not on the whole found the same results as did Seligman and his associates. This may be for a number of reasons to do with the experimental situation itself, rather than because uncontrollable outcomes have no effect on people's motivations and levels of activity. For one thing, given the widespread belief that events are not random but controllable, it is difficult to make subjects believe that there *really* is no contingency between their behaviour and their outcomes. Then 'helplessness' in human subjects is usually assessed, not by subjects not responding at all, but by their performance on another task. Furthermore, as Wortman has pointed out, a lot depends on whether or not the subjects expected to have control over the outcomes, and whether the outcomes were important to them. If they expect to have some control over important outcomes, and if there is a little evidence of potential control, they become the opposite of 'helpless', and try frantically to reassert control. It is only when the first two conditions hold and they find that there is absolutely no possibility of control that their behaviour fits the original Seligman model (Wortman and Brehm, 1975).

However, in a number of studies in natural settings absence of control over events has been shown to result in stress manifested in illness as well as in behaviour. For example, in one study residents in an old people's home who received volunteer visitors were divided into two groups. In one the residents could make their own visiting arrangements and in the other they could not. There were marked effects on the health and morale of the group without control (Schultz, 1976) (the use of subjects on a non-voluntary basis for the testing of procedures which may affect their well-being is unusual and to be deplored). In another study incoming residents to another old people's home were asked in a questionnaire about the degree of choice they felt that they had had about living in the home or elsewhere. The mortality rate of those with the lowest reported sense of choice (or least sense of control over their fate) was significantly higher than amongst those with a greater sense of choice (Ferrare, 1962). It should be clear from these few accounts that a sense of self as an agent, that is a sense of control over one's outcomes, contributes to a sense of oneself as an agent and is critical for many aspects of adjustment.

Another approach to the study of the self as agent has been concerned with the effects of attempts to limit people's freedom to choose their own courses of action. This research has been generated within the framework provided by Brehm's theory of psychological reactance. In essence this theory states that when people perceive some barrier, personal or impersonal, to their freedom to choose a course of action they will act to restore their sense of freedom. Put in the terms already used in this chapter, we can call this freedom 'a sense of self as an agent'. Brehm puts it in this way: 'It is assumed that people have the subjective experience of freedom to do what they want, to do it in the way they want, and to do it when they want in regard to limited and specifiable areas of behavior' (Brehm, 1966, p. 118). As we have seen, lack of control over outcomes is one kind of loss of freedom, which has aversive effects on people's well-being, and Brehm in his theory puts forward some other sources of loss of freedom.

One source is another person's attempt to influence our actions, for example when a shop assistant attempts to persuade us to buy one item rather than another, or when someone tries to convince us of their views, or more subtly when they do us some kind of unsolicited favour which makes us feel constrained to return it. The dependence of others is a threat because we have internalized views that we should help those in need, and when someone dependent on us for help asks for it our freedom either to help or not to help is threatened. Even our own predilections and habits or strong preferences can be a source of reactance; for example an addiction to smoking can be a constraint on our freedom to go without cigarettes and spend the money on something else, that is in so far as the desire is beyond our perceived control. Sometimes threats are impersonal as when some previously available items become unavailable.

Psychological reactance is the state of mind that people experience under any of these circumstances, which according to Brehm will activate people to try and restore their freedom, either directly or indirectly through expressions of hostility towards the person or thing that is implicated in their loss of freedom. A number of subtle experiments have illustrated reactance effects. In one, for example, student subjects were asked to fill in a questionnaire concerned with their views on lowering the voting age. They were led to expect that they were to hear a talk from a speaker who supported the generally held position in favour of lowering the voting age. In one condition of the experiment the subjects were told that the talk had been cancelled because the college administration had decided that it would be wrong for them to hear a talk favouring the lowering of the voting age (this was the censorship condition). The others were told that the talk would be cancelled because of the speaker's illness (no censorship condition). Their attitudes towards the issue were then measured again, and it was found that the group in the censorship condition (presumed by the authors to be the one arousing psychological reactance) showed a much more extreme move towards the speaker's position than those in the no-censorship condition (Wicklund and Brehm, 1967). In another, similar experiment it was found that subjects showed themselves to be influenced more when they 'overheard' a speaker putting forward a particular point of view than when the speaker was presented as *trying* to influence them (Walster and Festinger, 1962).

Yet others have examined the effect of arbitrarily removing an item, for example a candy bar or a toy, from an array from which the subjects were expecting to be able to choose, and have found that the item removed gained in attractiveness for the subjects irrespective of whether or not it was highly valued in the first place.

One experiment (Schwarz, 1970) illustrated how another's dependence (even an unknown other) could be felt as a threat to freedom and produce reactance effects. This experiment utilized the standard charity-appeal situation, the demand in this case being for bone-marrow donors for a transplant patient. The recipient was presented as being either in great need (reactance condition), moderate need or slight need, and the likelihood of the subject being suitable for donorship was similarly varied. Both these factors together should have affected the amount of pressure felt by the potential donors to comply with the appeal. Both the experiment and its findings were complex, but it emerged that the response rate dropped where the need was perceived to be great and the likelihood of being suitable increased, that is individuals would feel more constrained to contribute. This experiment illustrated one of the problems of demonstrating reactance effects. Clearly, in the situation outlined above people feel on the one hand a wish to help and comply with a request, but the threat to freedom produces a desire not to – that is, a conflict. Reactance is thus measured by the decrease in response from that which might be normally expected (given people's reasonable charity). The difficulty, methodologically speaking, is in assessing what level of compliance might have been expected in order to assess the degree of reactance. From all these experiments we can see that reactance produces some kind of negative behaviour, but of course that behaviour does not in itself necessarily restore people's freedom either real or imagined. However, Worchel and Brehm (1971) argue that these negative or aggressive responses to loss of freedom are the necessary conditions for people actually to move towards restoring it.

Reactance theory is just another approach to studying the importance of the perception of self as an agent. How does it relate to the work on the effects of lack of control over outcomes? Worchel and Brehm argue that basically when people feel their control diminished or threatened (as in the reactance situations just described) they will react with anger or in one of the ways we have already encountered. If, however, they are confronted with complete loss of control over what happens to them they will react with 'helplessness' or passivity (Wortman and Brehm, 1975). The critical point here is that perception of self as an effective agent is important and therefore has implications for our dealings with other people, both in terms of allowing them a sense of power and freedom and in enhancing our own sense of agency in order to realize our goals with others.

Beliefs in control and the importance of freedom are shared by everybody, but in varying degrees even within our own culture. We have to remember that we live in a culture where choice and individual freedom (real or illusory) are highly valued, and it is because they are highly valued that they are studied at all. After all, psychology is constructed by people, themselves products of value and belief systems, and the scientific endeavour has to be relative to this fact. We must remember, therefore, that in non-consumer, non-capitalist societies this particular experience of self may figure less importantly in human affairs than it does in ours. However, within our own context individuals vary in the degree to which they feel themselves free and in control.

The attempt to measure an individual's beliefs about control were initiated some years ago by Rotter (1966), and the resulting scale was called the internal–external (I–E) locus of control scale. The items in it are concerned with beliefs about the degree to which events across a variety of domains, work, politics, personal happiness, interpersonal relations are determined by one's own actions or by factors outside one's control like luck. Look at the following pairs of statements:

1 Many of the unhappy things in people's lives are due partly to bad luck.
2 People's misfortunes result from the mistakes they make.

1 Getting a good job depends mainly on being in the right place at the right time.
2 Becoming a success is a matter of hard work, luck has nothing to do with it.

The first of each of these pairs of statements suggests a belief that one has little control over events, the second of each pair that one has indeed some control over events. From a number of such pairs of statements people are asked to tick the one which most closely reflects their belief, and their overall score characterizes their locus-of-control orientation as either internal (events affected by one's own behaviour) or external (events affected by unpredictable factors external to oneself).

Rotter argued that the orientation that an individual develops results from experience, in particular whether the outcomes or results of one's actions have been randomly related to the actions or whether there has been a pattern of contingency between one's actions and the outcomes. For example, in school settings hard work and good behaviour may be rewarded with praise and attention, or with being ignored, or with being criticized in an apparently random fashion. Such a situation should lead to an individual having an external locus of control (at least with respect to the school setting), whereas good performance rewarded and bad performance unrewarded should lead to a sense of internal control. Rotter's idea is very similar to the work on learned helplessness discussed earlier, only in this case Rotter is arguing that lack of control over events leads to a generalized belief system (Rotter, 1966). However, this in itself should have implications for behaviour, and research carried out to validate the I–E scale (that is demonstrate that it measures what it is supposed to be measuring) suggests that people with an external orientation do behave more passively (helplessly) than those with an internal orientation. For example, in one study long-stay patients in a sanatorium were classified on the basis of Rotter's scale. Those who were internal in locus of control had sought more information about their medical conditions, the nature of the treatment they were receiving and the workings of the hospital than those classified as external (Seeman and Evans, 1962). Other studies have shown internals to be more able or willing to exert self-control; for example internals are more able than externals to give up smoking when they decide to. Not surprisingly, internals are more likely to be successful academically, since belief in personal efficacy allows people to set realistic and achievable goals, raising their aspirations when they experience success, and also to postpone reward so that they can set themselves long-term goals. In general, higher-status people (who after all have the opportunity to exercise more power over events than low-status people do) show up as higher in internal locus of control (Phares, 1976).

It should be clear from this that internal locus of control is a more valued orientation than external locus (just as apparent freedom of choice and action are), and perhaps a word should be said about this. Presumably it is adaptive to believe in internal control where there is a reasonable degree of evidence for its existence. Some events, like aeroplane crashes, are not under the control of the victims. The capacity of poverty-stricken, ailing peasants in right-wing police states to improve their personal situations is extremely limited. It would not be psychologically adaptive to take responsibility for these events and states of affairs, in the sense of attributing their causes to one's personal actions, since the ensuing sense of failure would likely lead to extreme loss of self-esteem and to depression. On the other hand, locus-of-control beliefs may become generalized to areas where some control is possible, and in this way produce fulfilling prophecies. People who have no belief in personal efficacy do little or nothing to affect their outcomes, thereby reinforcing their belief that what happens to them is determined by outside forces, thus reinforcing their passivity, and so on.

We have seen three areas of research concerned with the perception of self as subject or agent and its implications for behaviour and adjustment. How might it affect social interaction and social relationships? A sense of agency and freedom is valued by most people, even if they do not feel they have much of either. Harmonious relationships depend not only on maintaining this experience for oneself but also on allowing the possibility for others. Unfortunately, some people enhance their own sense of power and control over relations with other people at the expense of the latter's power and control. And yet passivity in others can also be extremely hard to tolerate. People who do not 'earn their psychological keep', who never provide the topic of conversation, never suggest a course of action, simply go along with everyone else, like puppets, can be extremely trying. We should all have an interest in some level of agency for everyone with whom we are involved. The problem is one of calibration (as it so often is in human affairs), finding that optimal point where all people can exercise their sense of freedom and control to their and everyone else's maximum benefit. As we shall see, a number of strategies for optimizing realistically the individual's sense of power have been devised for therapeutic ends and have a place in social-skills training.

Let us now turn to some other aspects of self-knowledge and self-interpretation. In the previous chapter we examined processes involved in understanding other people, that is understanding the causes of their behaviours and their underlying dispositions.

We shall now focus on a parallel process, namely that involved in understanding ourselves. We shall consider the process at a number of levels: how we interpret information arising out of bodily states or partly out of bodily states, information to do with pain and discomfort and to do with emotional states; how we locate the causes of our own behaviour; what schemata we employ in understanding ourselves as characters; how we evaluate ourselves; and the extent to which beliefs about self become self-fulfilling prophecies.

Interpreting information from bodily states

It is something of a mystery how we learn to talk about internal states in a way which is meaningful to others at all. Consider children. When children learn language they learn to apply linguistic labels for things in roughly the same way as the adult users of language in that community apply them. Thus they will observe people using the word 'dog' in the presence of lots of different sorts of dogs, and they will apply the word themselves sometimes correctly and sometimes not, receiving feedback from adults about their correctness. But no adult language-user can see inside other people's heads and correct them for their use of the word 'hurts' or for the use of the phrase 'I feel sick'. The adult may have other information in both those cases, from how the child is acting and looking and from what it has just been doing, but nevertheless can only hazard rough guesses. Even more problematic is the case of acquiring labels for emotional states. However do children learn to use words like 'depressed', 'bored', 'angry'? The data for adults providing the feedback is again the children's behaviour and the circumstances in which that behaviour has occurred, but this process is highly inferential. Children's acquisition of labels for their feelings, therefore, is highly dependent on the inferences of those around them, that is on attributions about the causes of behaviour, in this case verbal behaviour.

Clearly there is enormous scope for individual variation in the capacity to label internal states and plenty of scope for people to acquire very idiosyncratic ways of doing it. One person can grow up identifying every faint discomfort as a nasty pain, and another be unable to identify quite serious internal traumas. People can grow up saying they are hungry when they are bored, or depressed, and depressed when they are actually tired, and so forth. Individuals vary in their awareness of their bodily states and the amount of attention they give to their own feelings and other events that are internal and unobservable by other people. Methods of measuring this individual variation in self-awareness have been developed by Miller *et al.* (1981) in the form of a scale to measure consciousness of body. This measure is concerned with people's awareness of bodily functions. Another (Fenigstein *et al.*, 1975), mentioned above, is concerned with self-consciousness of one's psychological states, concern with how one appears to others and vulnerability to self-conscious anxiety.

The perception of pain is in itself an extremely interesting psychological problem, but it is less central to our current concern, which is that of feelings relevant to social interaction. Therefore, we shall here look at the perception of emotional states, since feelings enter quite strongly into our behaviour with other people.

Emotional states involve bodily changes and thoughts. The bodily changes are largely changes to do with states of arousal, that is changes in heart rate, blood pressure, skin conductance, and a whole range of other changes which are variously detectable to people. They are controlled by the action of the autonomic nervous system, and they get the body into a state of readiness to take action. In some emotional states the physiological changes are quite dramatic, as in extreme fear or rage or sexual arousal. In others they are quite slight as in generalized euphoria or faint nostalgia. Psychologists are not entirely in agreement about the extent to which physiological changes are really different in such different states as anger and fear and sexual arousal, and whether, if they are different, they are perceptibly different. Schachter (1964), for example, does not believe that there are easily discriminable physiological differences among the different emotional states. Others believe that particular patterns of physiological activity do become associated with particular states within the individual and provide important input for individuals in deciding what they feel (Izard, 1977). But perception of bodily states is only one component of the information that leads us to describe ourselves as feeling one emotion rather than another. Perhaps rather more immediate are our perceptions of our thoughts. We can perceive the difference between feeling angry and feeling frightened because our apprehension of situations informs us of the difference. Many psychologists, concerned with self-management techniques of personal change, believe that thought processes are crucial in initiating and sustaining feelings, and that if we want to change our feelings we need to interrupt and change our thoughts. We shall see examples of such techniques in chapter 9.

Then there is information from expressive reactions, that is from facial movements, teeth-clenching, stiff upper lips, etc., the elements that were discussed in the chapter on non-verbal communication (chapter 5). Some psychologists argue that these muscular changes provide input to our understanding of our feelings and indeed can anticipate the thoughts and labels which finally crystallize them. Thus the discovery of a clenched fist does finally convince us that we are indeed very angry.

Finally there is information from the social context, the situation, the behaviour of others present, the normativeness of one emotion rather than another, and so on, so that, for example, a funeral is sufficient to add conviction to our melancholy mood.

For some years psychological thinking about emotional processes has been dominated by an attributional model. This model assumes that emotion is not experienced 'directly', which is how most of us think of it, but is experienced as the outcome of a complex process of inference in which the information from various sources is weighed up. Much of this work has been concerned with the relative weighting given to physiological cues on the one hand and social-contextual cues on the other. For example, in a famous study, Schachter and Singer (1962) induced the physiological symptoms of emotional arousal in their subjects by giving them a drug whose action is similar to that of adrenaline. They all thought they were participating in an experiment concerned with the effects of that drug on visual perception. Some were told correctly about the 'side effects' (that is the symptoms of emotional arousal), others were told nothing, and others again were told incorrectly of quite different symptoms. While they waited for the 'experiment' to begin they were joined by another 'subject' (actually a confederate of the experimenter) who either acted in an angry and disagreeable manner or (in the other conditions) in a boisterously euphoric manner. Schachter and Singer argued that where they had no reason to attribute their adrenaline-created emotional arousal to the drug, they would have to attribute it to other factors, in particular to the atmosphere created by the stooge's behaviour, and this attribution would create in them the emotion. The results suggested that in conditions where subjects had no ready explanation for how they were feeling they used cues from the environment to label their experiences.

This model provided the basis for a great deal of research. Schachter himself applied it to problems of obesity and overeating, his idea being that some obese people misinterpret their internal cues to hunger and/or become excessively dependent on external cues, like the appearance of food or the demands of social occasions, and eat when they are not actually hungry. It has been used as an explanation of romantic heterosexual attachments. Here the idea is that the generalized arousal associated with the early stages of sexual arousal, but in fact produced by, for example, an anxiety-provoking situation occurring in the presence of a suitable partner and appropriate setting, will lead to strong attraction, since the arousal will be attributed to the qualities of the partner and situation (Dutton and Aron, 1974). The model is however useful only where we can assume both that the physiological information is, in fact, vague and diffuse (and as suggested above, a number of psychologists dispute this) and that the other input from one's thoughts is absent. Intuitively, it seems, people usually have quite strong input from these thoughts. Certainly, from clinical studies concerned with modifying states of fear and anxiety and depression, thought processes seem to play a highly influential role in experiencing emotion. In the Schachter and Singer experiments the physiological arousal was induced by a drug. Normally however our appreciation of situations produces this arousal. The prospect of taking an important examination is sufficient to produce arousal symptoms of fear. A gratuitous insult from a colleague suffices to produce the arousal necessary for anger. The puzzle is why people get aroused by particular things. People react quite differently in terms of arousal. In fact there are two things to explain: one of them is to do with the emotional lability of some people and the unresponsiveness of others; the other is to do with varying individual response to situations. The psychodynamic tradition stresses that the only way to answer the second question is through extensive exploration of what particular situations and stimuli have come to mean to people. More recent traditions stress the importance of actually changing physiological reactions and thoughts, without necessarily having to understand either. All this will be dealt with later. The major focus for us here is whether or not emotional responses are modifiable since they affect our behaviour with others.

Locating the causes of our own behaviour

In the previous chapter it was suggested that one of the standards against which one might attempt to judge the accuracy of someone's judgement about another might be that individual's judgement of himself or herself. Common sense leads us to believe that we all know more about ourselves than other people can possibly do, and that the information we have at our disposal is complete. In this and the next section we shall present evidence that we are not necessarily more correct in our judgements about ourselves than we are in our judgements about others. Obviously the information that we have at our disposal is different and our attention is quite differently focused according to whether we are judging ourselves or judging others.

A number of studies have documented the fact that we often explain the behaviour of others through the use of internal attributions, that is we refer to personality traits, whereas when providing explanations of our own behaviour we use external causes or at least refer to the situation in which the behaviour occurs (Goldberg, 1978). The reasons put forward for this difference in causal attribution have focused on the two factors of information and attention. Observers and actors have different information available to them. In particular actors know how much their behaviour has varied in the past and therefore they are unlikely to see their present behaviour as necessarily a typical and representative sample of their behaviour in general (in terms of the Kelley model they would be assuming low consistency). The observer makes a general (and usually erroneous) assumption (Nisbett and Ross, 1980), that is an assumption of high consistency, and therefore sees present behaviour as reflecting an enduring trait. Then, as we saw in the last chapter, the salience or vividness of particular information gives that information priority in the eyes of the observer searching for causes. To actors, whose attentions are necessarily directed outwards, it is the situation which is likely to be more salient. To observers focusing on the actor, it is the latter who is the more vivid and salient and therefore claims attention as a possible cause (Nisbett *et al.*, 1973). The main point is that we are not aware of *all* the information that we may in fact be processing and responding to. There is an abundance of evidence showing that we cannot necessarily give verbal reports of stimuli which from other evidence it is clear that we are responding to: that is, we can process and respond without awareness. This research has been for the most part concerned with non-personal information (Erdelyi, 1974).

But let us look now at some research which has been concerned with judgements about the causes of our own behaviour, or our own internal states. In a series of experiments Nisbett and Wilson (1977a, 1977b) asked subjects to make judgements about various stimuli under circumstances in which the experimenters could easily influence those judgements and indeed prove that they had influenced them. Yet subjects rarely spotted the factors which had influenced them. In one of these studies, in which subjects watched a video-taped interview with a lecturer about his work and his students, the lecturer had a very strong foreign accent. Half the subjects saw him talking in a highly agreeable manner; the others saw him behaving in an extremely disagreeable manner. All subjects had to rate the instructor on his likeableness (which clearly varied under the two conditions) and on his physical appearance, mannerisms and accent (which were invariant across the two conditions). Not surprisingly the 'nice' group rated him as much more likeable than the 'nasty' group did. The 'nice' group also rated his mannerisms, etc., as attractive, the 'nasty' group rated mannerisms, etc., as unattractive (thus demonstrating a 'halo' effect). Half the subjects were asked if the mannerisms, etc., had influenced their ratings of the lecturer as a person; the other half were asked if their ratings of the lecturer as a person had influenced their ratings of the mannerisms, etc. Although it was clear to the observers that attributes like manner and accent were perceived as attractive in a pleasant person and unattractive in an unpleasant person, the subjects, especially in the 'nasty' condition, reported that their dislike of the mannerisms and accent had made them dislike the person. Thus it was clear that people did not understand the real causes of their *own* judgements.

In another study subjects were shown a film either under normal conditions or under distracting conditions (half of them saw the film with a very loud noise coming from outside, and the other half with the film out of focus). Subjects then had to rate the film in terms of general interests, its likely impact on other people and how sympathethic they found the main characters. The ratings were as favourable amongst the groups who saw the film under poor conditions as they were amongst those who saw it under proper conditions. The experimenter then apologized for the poor viewing conditions and asked subjects to indicate next to each of their ratings whether the rating had in fact been influenced by the poor conditions. In reality the poor conditions had had absolutely no effect on the ratings. However, the subjects in the noise condition reported that the noise had in fact lowered their ratings of the film. These studies seem to demonstrate that people can be quite wrong about the actual influence on their behaviours. However, in these cases the behaviours are trivial and not likely to recur. Certain kinds of behaviour which one might classify as habits or liabilities or automatic routines are behaviours where immediate causes escape our awareness. For example we know why *in general* we feel the need to smoke or eat, but the subtle conditioned link between environmental cues, particular behavioural sequences and the lighting up of a particular cigarette is likely to escape our notice. Of course it might be that people search more carefully for information having a bearing on causes of important and recurring things.

The next study is concerned with the perception of influences on mood. Weiss and Brown (1977) asked subjects to keep a daily record of their moods over a two-month period. They were also asked to keep a track of several factors that might have influenced their moods, like weather, amount of sleep each night, general health, day of the week, sexual activity, and so on. At the end of the two months the subjects were asked to indicate how important they thought these factors had generally been on their own moods. The investigators were able to show the actual statistical relationships between each of the factors and mood. They also found that there was little relationship between what the subjects thought were factors and what, statistically speaking, were factors. For example the researcher found that day of the week was strongly related to subjects' reports of mood. But subjects themselves reported 'sleep' as being the most important factor (in fact it was relatively unimportant!). Why might people be so unaware of true relationships between influencing variables and their own behaviour? One likely reason is the existence of causal schemata like the ones discussed in the last chapter. Subjects, whether they are trying to ascertain the causes of other people's or their own behaviour are fairly dependent on their own theories of likely causes, which may lead them to ignore information which is incongruent with the theory. Of course when it comes to even more complex courses of action, and actions which strongly involve the ego of the actor, differential attention to certain factors may well be motivated by self-interest. For example an individual who, for unfathomable reasons, has lurched from one type of occupation to another and one way of life to another may 'see' in his or her 'career' a pattern of development, such that each change with hindsight makes sense and could have been predicted, and also makes sense in terms of some recently discerned goal. The pattern one sees in such long-spanned events is highly dependent on the theory one has of how events are linked. For example, in studies of women who became bisexual or homosexual the accounts they gave of their slightly deviant life styles showed a clear effect of some popular theories about the origins of lesbianism, for example unfortunate or exploitative relationships with men, and so forth (Blumstein and Schwarz, 1977). People who are particularly adept at constructing such patterns of causal links are those trained in psychoanalytic theory, whether as practitioners or as clients. As Nisbett and Ross (1980) have remarked, there is little basis for knowing whether these patterns exist really in the minds of the practitioners or in the lives of the client.

One must perhaps point out, however, that in searching for the causes of their own behaviours actors do have access to certain important data. First actors know what factors in the environment mean to them. For example the wave of nostalgia that a visit to a bleak mining village brings is a function of the meanings of the area for the individual and are not detectable through objective features perceived by the observer. Second actors can fit their present behaviour into a whole schema of plans which the observer is unaware of. It is not surprising that actors give different accounts of the causes of their actions to those given by observers. The knotty problem is that of knowing where the approximate truth lies, and whether actions really have 'a cause', or 'many causes', or indeed no causes at all!

In the previous chapter we spoke of schemata as relatively fixed theories about the structure of personality through which we filter information about others and with which we represent particular others to ourselves. This is shown both in the phenomenon of seeing the causes of other people's actions within their dispositions rather than in their situations, and in the way in which we feel able to characterize those whom we know well and to predict their behaviour. Whether our schemata about ourselves are as stable is less clear. Given that actors often give situational reasons for their actions, we might imagine that we have many self-schemata which relate to different situations. Thus we might have a picture of a relaxed self on holiday, of a rigid, responsible self at work, of a generous and reliable self to one's family, and so forth. This is particularly likely to be so if, as many social theorists believe, our self-conceptions are social in origin, that is, they are brought about by the attitudes and behaviours of others towards us. Think of the female at the end of the telephone in the Snyder, Tanke and Berscheid study (1977), presented in the previous chapter. Her partner behaved towards her as if she were attractive, and so others saw her acting as if she were attractive. Given some reasonable degree of exposure to these kinds of assumptions, one can imagine that she would have developed a schema for herself in that situation which revolved around the idea of herself as attractive. However, imagine her then moving to the situation of the female in the unattractive condition, which in real life she could quite easily do; that is she could find herself in a situation where no one present thinks of her as attractive, as the situation does not allow her to act as attractive. Presumably she would have two situation-specific self-schemata.

The number of situationally based self-schemata that people have must depend in part on the variability of their own behaviour and the variation in other people's conceptions of them. The possibility of multiple self-schemata is a phenomenon of those societies in which most people have to cope with an array of quite different situations and where the prescriptions for how to act are various. In a simple, static society a person's social identity is limited by the fact that few roles are available and performance in most of them is visible to everyone else.

In our own society there are in addition stages in the life cycle where a person's self-schema is likely to be unstable. For example the expectations of some adolescents by other people are varied, and the roles that they could adopt and the models available for the adoption of those roles are extremely diverse. Such conditions make the development of a single, stable self-schema difficult to achieve, and the difficulty may be experienced as an 'identity crisis' (Erikson, 1968). Adolescence is not the only life stage where a weakening of one's self-schema may be threatened: marriage, parenthood, retirement, serious illness, all can produce the same effect. Also, life stages are not the only conditions which may threaten integrated self-schemata. Confused and ambivalent family relationships during childhood, confusion about one's sexual preferences, the absence of any very clear talents or abilities may hinder the emergence of a consistent self-schema.

Over-concern about others' opinions and the demands of social situations may also undermine a person's sense of what he or she is really like. Some of these potential sources of hindrance to a stable self-concept can be measured. For example, individuals vary in their susceptibility to embarrassment (remember that that is produced by the awareness of a discrepancy between some publicly claimed identity and the facts emerging in the situation). One might suppose that people who are easily embarrassed would be aware of discrepancies between public and private self. Modigliani developed a questionnaire aimed at assessing people's perceptions of their own vulnerability to embarrassment. The questionnaire consists of twenty-six items referring to situations which are known to be embarrassing, and individuals are asked to rate the likely level of their own embarrassment in each situation (Modigliani, 1968). Another approach to individual variation in susceptibility to such social influence has been that of Snyder (1974). He suggested that people vary in the degree to which they are aware of situational demands and the degree to which they monitor their own behaviour in public in order to fit these demands. The self-monitoring scale is a twenty-five-item scale in which people endorse statements as being applicable to them. The statements include the following:

I would probably make a good actor.
In different situations and with different people I often act like very different persons.

I may deceive people by being friendly when I really dislike them.

These measures are of course concerned only with factors which might lower the stability of a person's self-schema. They don't concern the content of self-schemata. However, it is just as possible to measure people's self-schemata as it is to measure their implicit theories of personality. That is people can provide self-descriptions and the stability of these over time can be examined. McGuire *et al.* (1979) found that in people's spontaneous self-descriptions the most prominent features were those that distinguished them from others around them – for example being male if one was describing self as a member of an otherwise female household, black if one was in a class of white children, stupid if one was with very intelligent people, and so forth. One of the problems of eliciting self-statements, however, is that they are likely to be vulnerable to social desirability and self-presentation effects. That is, if asked to give an account of oneself as a person, that account is likely not only to be biased towards socially desirable traits but also towards a greater level of consistency than is 'really' the case (we cannot hope ever to be any more precise about that 'really' in the case of oneself than we are when it concerns judgements of others). What would be interesting, though extremely difficult, to do would be to obtain self-descriptive statements under conditions in which individuals did not know that they were the focus of interest. Most people's spontaneous self-descriptive statements emerge in casual conversations, which it is difficult for the investigator to overhear. But were it available, one could carry out on that data the kind of multi-dimensional scaling that was carried out on Theodore Dreiser's fictional characters, as described in chapter 6.

One study of self-schemata has been undertaken by Markus (1977). She used as evidence for a strong self-schema extreme ratings on a particular dimension, that of independence–dependence. She found that on a subsequent test of 'suggestibility', those with extreme self-ratings failed to process information which was inconsistent with their self-conceptions, thus demonstrating that self-schemata can influence information processing. However, one weakness of this study is that *extremity* of rating on a dimension is considered evidence for a self-schema. There is no reason to suppose that a self-schema cannot consist of ideas about having characteristics in moderate amounts. It was suggested in the previous chapter that implicit personality theories exert an influence on the ways in which we attend to information and recall it, that is both processes are biased towards information which is congruent with the theory, even though we know little about the schemata themselves. We have some evidence that the same process operates with self-schemata. Swann and Read (1981) gave a group of subjects various measures of self-concept, including self-esteem, and put them into groups in which they would be interacting with others who either liked or disliked them. They were told that they could read the actual evaluations others had made of them. The investigators observed how long the subjects spent reading the evaluations. They found that the most time was taken by those who evaluated themselves positively, reading statements from others who also evaluated them positively, and by those who disliked themselves, reading statements from others who had evaluated them negatively. In a subsequent study using the same procedure, the subjects had to spend a few moments interacting with the person who had evaluated them, and these conversations were rated by judges for evidence of subjects eliciting congruent behaviour from the others. The authors concluded that the data illustrated the process whereby people use social interaction as a way of eliciting feedback which verifies their self-conceptions.

Self-evaluation and self-esteem

Perhaps the most important dimension of the way that we think about ourselves is that of evaluation, that is our level of self-esteem. The degree to which we globally approve of ourselves has an impact on how we behave, particularly with other people.

To a certain degree our evaluations of ourselves are dependent on comparisons with other people. For example in judging specific abilities our judgements can really only be relative: the question of how good a tennis player/musician/cook/beauty contestant one is is only meaningful with reference to a scale derived from other people's performances. There is ample evidence that we look for opportunities to compare ourselves with relevant others. By relevant we mean others who are likely to be sufficiently close to us in terms of some overall scale for the comparison to be meaningful. For example, the local tennis club provides a more meaningful set of comparisons about our tennis skills than international championships would. In fact the widespread interest in competitions in everything from beauty to general knowledge suggests that people are interested in trying to establish population norms and the top and bottom anchors to scales. We simply cannot answer the question of how generous we have been in giving money to a charity, for example, unless we have at least the following information:

How much the largest amount given was.
How much the smallest amount given was.
How much most people gave.
How many people gave at all.

The group that one chooses as one's point of comparison is called a reference group. In our society we have a wide choice of such comparison groups, and whether we choose to compare ourselves with people who are slightly 'better' or slightly 'worse' than ourselves will have considerable impact on our evaluations of our own abilities and subsequently on our self-esteem. In using others for comparison we are inevitably involved in attributional processes. For example, in judging someone's achievement in a given field one has to assess the situational factors which could have facilitated or hindered that achievement. People with generally low self-esteem tend to attribute the successes of others to internal factors and their failures to external factors, while they judge their own successes as due to situational factors and their failures to internal factors (Ickes and Laydon, 1978). Both the selection of reference groups and how we attribute other people's and our own achievements will relate to self-esteem. What is not clear is whether self-esteem is brought about by these judgements or the judgements are brought about by the general need to maintain a *consistent* level of self-esteem, high or low.

People vary in their global level of self-esteem and this variation can be measured. One scale that has been developed for this purpose is that of Rosenberg (1965), who asked people to indicate their level of agreement with ten items, of which the following are a sample:

I certainly feel useless at times.
On the whole I am satisfied with myself.

Rosenberg found that people who showed low self-esteem on this scale showed the following characteristics: they received independent ratings from others as very much more miserable and easily discouraged; they were much less active and involved in social situations than were people with high self-esteem (one would expect that people with low self-esteem would not feel confident that others would value their contributions and therefore they would be much more reluctant to make any); people with low self-esteem thought others evaluated them poorly in general; they felt awkward with others and, avoiding social contact, ended up feeling isolated and lonely. Low self-esteem is a common factor in depression and often in anxiety as well. Once again we have to recall the argument that it is not possible to establish a standard for judging whether a person's self-evaluation is accurate or not, since in this everything depends on the implicit comparison that is being made. Nevertheless we tend to think of low self-esteem as a distortion of judgement and high self-esteem as more veridical. But this is not necessarily so. One study (Lewinsohn and Mischel, 1980) suggests that high self-esteem is an adaptive position taken up even though it may have little basis. The authors compared the judgements of social competence that members of groups gave each other and themselves. Those individuals who had been classified as depressed (depression is almost defined by low self-esteem) rated their own social competence more poorly than the non-depressed subjects did. However, their ratings of themselves were much closer to the ratings that others gave them than were the ratings of the non-depressed subjects. The latter continually over-estimated themselves in comparison with others' estimations of them. However, the authors point out that veridical perceptions of oneself may generally do more harm than good! When we consider self-fulfilling prophecies in relation to the self-concept, we shall consider this point again.

Effects of beliefs about self on behaviour

People's beliefs about themselves get translated into behaviour and that behaviour may in itself produce the feedback that confirms the beliefs. This is the self-fulfilling prophecy process that was discussed in the last chapter. Some evidence of it was suggested in the study by Swann and Read (1981), described above (p. 121). Perhaps the most fully investigated effects of the self-fulfilling nature of beliefs about the self are those concerned with personal efficacy. At the beginning of this chapter it was pointed out that the belief that you can control your own outcomes has direct effects on your efforts to do so, as well as effects on your psychological and physical well-being. We also have more general evidence that beliefs that we can succeed at tasks influence the likelihood of success, independently of all the other factors which are responsible for success. Beliefs that one is likely to succeed are dependent partly on one's experience of success in the past. In a series of studies Feather (1965, 1966) showed that prior success increases one's belief that one will succeed in the future and prior failure decreases one's belief in future success. This of course holds only if one attributes the causes of success and failure to internal factors. These beliefs get translated into effort and result in the finding that people with a belief in their own efficacy are more likely to achieve goals which another person without that belief, and even with greater ability, will not achieve. Naturally every achievement feeds into the prior level of success and raises the subjective probability of success on the next occasion, resulting in the often cited lay person's law that 'success breeds success'. Most of the work on the self-fulfilling properties of beliefs about the self have derived from experimental studies involving performance on simple tasks. This has been so because it is clearly necessary to eliminate all the factors which also account for success like ability, opportunity, experience. But it needs no great imaginative leap to believe that the beliefs that one is witty, kind, dull, sparkling or whatever will result in behaviours and interactions which will make those beliefs become true. And the evidence from the study by Swann and Read mentioned earlier reinforces the idea that we try actively to get others to behave in ways which accord with our main beliefs about ourselves. If we don't think much of ourselves we make it hard for other people to behave as if that poor evaluation were untrue.

Self-disclosure and social relationships

In earlier chapters we have alluded to the idea that people perceive an invisible boundary around themselves, which is physical in the form of that buffer zone we call personal space and psychological in that we restrict the access others have to information about us, including information which could, after all, for ever remain private because it derives from events inside our heads and bodies. At other points we have hinted at the possibility that people might be aware of, on the one hand, a publicly presented self and, on the other, a private self which is experienced as 'more authentic' and known only to intimates. We are going to conclude this chapter by looking briefly at the implications of people's willingness to reveal aspects of themselves.

Individual differences in willingness to reveal information about self across different domains, ranging from work (least intimate), through money and personality to body, have mostly been assessed by self-answering questionnaires (Jourard, 1971). Although these provide an estimate of people's usual level of willingness to self-disclose, they take little account of the situational, cultural and interpersonal factors which are equally important. For example people of higher status are less likely to disclose information about themselves to lower-status people than the other way round (Slobin *et al.*, 1968). Not surprisingly people disclose more to people they like than to people they dislike (Certier, 1970). People disclose more to their mothers than to their fathers, and more to women in general than to men (Jourard, 1971). Certain settings facilitate disclosure more than others do, and even such factors as physical proximity affect people's willingness to disclose (Goodstein and Reinecker, 1974).

For the most part self-disclosure is seen as a positive indicator of mental health (Rogers, 1961; Jourard, 1971). It is seen as implying trust and self-acceptance, and as reducing the potential for embarrassment and the need for defensiveness. Continuing to feel socially acceptable and viable when a reasonable number of other people know aspects of oneself which are often concealed is an important component of self-confidence. Since self-disclosure is often reciprocated, people who keep themselves very private are cut off from the feedback and insight that others' responses to their self-disclosures might provide. For example one often learns that features of one's private experience which one had found disturbing or shameful are by no means uncommon, and this is usually reassuring.

However, self-disclosure seems not to be favoured by certain conditions. For example, males in our society are often much more reluctant to disclose information about their feelings, and their ways of establishing intimacy with people who are close to them on other criteria are limited. But this could well be an adaptive response to the competitive and instrumental roles that men have to occupy, because occupation forms such a crucial part of their lives. Letting others know about one's weaknesses is not a smart move when one is in competition with them. All this suggests that understanding the advantages and disadvantages of self-disclosure would be an important aspect of social competence.

One important feature of self-disclosure in interaction is that it follows principles of exchange. That is if one person discloses information about himself or herself there appears to be a felt obligation on the part of the other to reciprocate, and this obligation is stronger in the early stages of a relationship than in the later stages (Altmann, 1972). This suggests the obvious tactic that if people wish to increase the intimacy of encounters in the sense of getting others to share more of themselves, it is necessary to volunteer self-disclosure themselves. In stable encounters this results in the participants matching the level of intimacy of their contributions, as they match so many other aspects of their behaviour (see chapters 4 and 5).

This chapter on awareness of self and its implications has been a long one. The justification lies in the importance of self, the central character and leading role in every performance, and a central component in happiness and in unhappiness. This importance will be further explored in the last section of the book.

8

Relationships and the exchange process

When we attempt to understand and enhance our interactions with other people it is not simply in order to bring off better social performances, it is also in order to improve our relationships with other people. A relationship is not just the sum total of all our interactions with someone, since the *ideas* and *wishes* which we entertain about another, quite independently of the frequency or the quality of our encounters with them, are factors in determining another's importance in our lives. Nevertheless interactions, particularly in the early stages of aquaintanceship, are the basic raw material.

Once again we have the problem of being at such an early stage in our scientific study of human affairs that we have no decent definition of the term 'relationship', and as professional psychologists we have to rely on using the term in much the same way as the lay person would. But what does it normally mean to us? Perhaps the term 'relationship' means 'contract'. When we have a relationship with someone, we mean that we have an implicit agreement to interact with them at some level of frequency and some level of intensity. Our agreement or contract may also implicitly specify that we each have rights and obligations, for example with respect to things like borrowing money or asking for help, exchanging presents, offering hospitality, being available even without prior appointment. The contract can be thought of as similar to a commercial contract, in which one party agrees to place orders of varying amounts and the other agrees to give that customer some priority in the supply. A single encounter with someone need have no past and no future, and can be likened to buying a loaf of bread in a bakers in a town which one has never visited before and is unlikely ever to visit again. A relationship is an agreement to trade, and the knowledge of that agreement remains at some level of awareness even though no transaction is actually going on at any particular moment.

This drift in metaphor towards the world of commerce is not inadvertent because it is in this chapter that we are going to consider social interaction, whether of the one-off variety or as a trading agreement, as a form of exchange. In considering it in this way we shall be making the assumptions that people evaluate their encounters with others, that they want to maximize their outcomes with other people, and that they have a fair degree of choice in both encounters and relationships. Thus we shall be looking at social interaction from a different perspective – that of the market place, where 'goods' and 'services' are exchanged. The simple economic theory of what determines the transactions in a market can be applied to social transactions too. We can set a value on any good or service (in the economic field this value is expressed in terms of money), we are all variously motivated to realize profits from our transactions, and we are all similarly free to enter into any transaction we wish. Later, of course, we shall see that these assumptions are not universally valid and extremely difficult to test empirically, but they do serve to introduce us to a very important feature of social life, which is that we *evaluate* the outcomes of our own and other people's behaviour. We saw earlier (chapter 7) that people need to believe that their behaviour has effects, and they want feedback about the relationship between a behaviour and its outcomes, otherwise they may become indecisive, helpless, depressed and generally ineffectual and unhappy. Now we are going further and asserting that people evaluate those outcomes and want the best that they can get.

The idea that people's behaviour is controlled by rewards is hardly radical in either professional or lay psychology. Common sense tells us that people strive for pleasure and avoid pain, and professional psychologists, one of the most eminent of whom was B.F. Skinner, have selected the controlling effects of reward or reinforcement as their central theme in understanding behaviour. One of the advances of social-exchange theory lies in the recognition that not only do we want rewards from others, but in order to get those rewards we have to dispense some ourselves, in short we have to learn how to be rewarding to others. In order to expand the metaphor, let us imagine a mini-market of four friends with time and behaviour to invest in each other and with bargains to be struck.

Adam has a number of friends, amongst whom are Bernadette, Catherine and David. According to a social-exchange view, the amount of time and trouble that Adam invests in each of them will be a function of the rewards and costs that each entails. The rewards that Bernadette offers are that she is a very willing listener and is prepared to sit it out while Adam circles round some personal, not very interesting, preoccupation of his own. Catherine cannot be relied upon to listen for any length of time, but on the other hand she is very entertaining with a good stock of funny stories. David is not a good listener nor is he particularly amusing, but he is very influential in the institution in which they both work and can be very helpful to Adam in all sorts of ways. So each of them has potential rewards for Adam if he 'invests' his behaviour in them. Social-exchange theory, however, does not take into account only the rewards of actions, but the costs of actions too. Profits consist of Rewards less Costs. Each of the three friends also have costs associated with them. For example, although Bernadette is a good listener, she rarely does anything else but listen, and Adam has to do all the conversational work. Catherine unfortunately lives a long distance away and has no car, and transportation is very poor in the area. If Adam wants to see Catherine he will have to incur the cost of driving there. David's problem is that his only source of conversation is the continual listing of his most recent achievements. Adam will have to calculate the benefit to him if he offsets the costs associated with each of them against the rewards. In exchange theory, Adam's decision to spend time with any one of them is a product of that calculation.

However, there is more to it than that. Because Adam has a choice and because (for argument's sake), he can only choose one of them, he is bound to forgo whatever profits were associated with any of those he didn't choose. Even if the profits were smaller, they still represent a further source of cost. When you buy a new car, part of the cost of that car is that you have forgone a holiday. So if Adam chooses to spend time with David, part of the cost of that is forgoing Bernadette's willingness to listen and Cathy's funny stories. The rest of the cost is contributed by those costs already associated with interaction with David and whatever time and effort is needed to see him.

You will notice immediately that rewards and costs can consist of all kinds of things and they can't really be compared with each other in terms of some common scale like money. With goods, we can say that a record is eight times the value of a packet of peanuts because their value is expressed in terms of the same currency. But we can't say that a joke is worth eight times being listened to for five minutes. Then (and of course this is true in the exchange of goods too) the value or cost of anything is subjectively defined and fluctuates from one time to another. A packet of peanuts would be more valuable than a record if you were hungry. A joke would be more valuable than a sympathetic ear if you had already spent two whole days talking about yourself. Then the value of anything is partly dependent on what you are used to in general. The value to someone of their first new car is different to the value of that same car to someone who already owns two. Just as the warmth of a spring day after winter seems greater than the heat of a normal summer day after a heatwave, so our evaluations of any outcome are dependent on a comparison level derived from past experience.

We can't, therefore, define precisely what constitutes rewards and costs because they depend on the tastes of the individual, and they depend on comparison levels, derived from that individual's experience. They certainly cannot be precisely quantified. Although this makes testing social-exchange theory difficult, it doesn't necessarily undermine its value as an approach to understanding human affairs. We *do* know of certain sources of rewards which are valued quite widely, for example compliments and approval, competence and confidence, physical attractiveness, and wide interests all contribute to how much people are generally liked by others; but of course they are not the only things, and for individuals their value would fluctuate according to needs and changing comparison levels.

We can distinguish two phases in the calculations of rewards and costs. One is the estimation phase; the other is the sampling phase. Before we know people well, for example at a party of strangers, we can only guess at the rewards and costs that they may entail, and our decisions to invest time and behaviour in them is based on an estimate. Even with people we do know well we can only guess what the rewards and costs will be on any particular occasion. Having made a decision, we begin to sample the rewards and costs in earnest. We may find that our profits turn out better than expected, or we may find that we have made a poor investment and are actually incurring a loss. What happens then? The social-exchange model suggests that in human affairs we continue to keep an eye on the market, that is we also have a comparison level for alternatives, which is determined by what we see as the profits potentially available in some other transaction or relationship. Should this comparison level for alternatives appear more profitable than what we are actually getting, we shall be motivated to leave the former encounter or relationship and set up the more profitable one.

So far we have talked about the problem of maximizing one's outcomes solely from the point of view of one party. In fact exchange means that both parties are involved. While Adam is doing his calculations, his three friends are doing theirs. Their encounters and relationships should turn out to be the ones which yield the best outcomes for both parties and exceed the comparison levels for alternatives for both parties. Thus social interaction should be a compromise, just as sales are compromises between buyers who think they have made the best purchases and sellers who think they have made the best sales in the prevailing circumstances. This compromise or reciprocity which lies at the heart of social exchange has important implications for us all. For not only do we have to concern ourselves with maximizing our own outcomes, but we have to be concerned with our partners' adequately ensuring their outcomes too, otherwise they will not do business and they will go elsewhere to alternative, more profitable ventures. Of course we have to admit that the 'perfect competition' assumption, where both parties are equally aware of their comparison levels for alternatives, and these levels are equally favourable, very often does not hold. People may become dependent on relationships because the alternatives are unsatisfactory, or because they don't realize what the alternatives are. We shall examine unequal relationships more closely a little later.

Applying these economic principles to understanding social interaction and social relationships introduces both a curious and apparently callous perspective on them. For example, normally we tend to talk about relationships in terms of liking, or having things in common, or 'getting on with' other people: we don't see ourselves as primarily into profiting from each other. Unfortunately the reasons we *give* for acting may not be the *actual* causes of our actions. The social-exchange theorist would suggest that we are not aware, necessarily, of calculating the profits derivable from other people, and the rhetoric we use to explain our transactions and relationships with others, both to other people and to ourselves, may have little bearing on the real factors involved, and our talk of liking, loving, 'being involved with', disliking or 'getting fed-up with' is just our way of making sense of our experiences of rewards and costs. Its apparent callousness contrasts with the rather moral perspectives we usually employ to talk about human relationships where our preferred values emphasize altruism and selflessness in our dealings with others. On the other hand, given the reciprocal nature of human exchange it may be that the social-exchange perspective provides a more substantial basis for arguing for real interdependence in relationships than does the rather shaky one of moral prescription, that is, if only we could realize it clearly, we are all actually interdependent. We don't need to argue that we all should be interdependent.

So far social-exchange theory is concerned with providing a framework for understanding people's choices in their transactions with others and the satisfaction in and stability of those transactions. It can take us further, however, into understanding some of the forms that relationships take, how relationships develop and dissolve.

A number of social scientists have put forward accounts of social behaviour based on exchange principles, of whom three of the most influential have been Homans, the sociologist, and Thibault and Kelley, the social psychologists. The latter have provided us in particular with an analytic tool, in the form of an outcome matrix, with which to explore some features of social transactions. In Figure 3 we have represented hypothetical situations. There are two actors, A and B, who have only two lines of action that they can carry out with each other, A1 and A2, and B1 and B2. Equally hypothetical are the values we have assigned to the results of those actions for the other (we have already explained that the task of actually quantifying outcomes is quite formidable). The numbers above the diagonal in each cell represent the value of A's outcomes for A in each contingency, and the numbers below the diagonal in each cell similarly represent the value of B's outcomes for B. The zero point would be set at the value of the comparison level for alternatives.

In figure 3(a) the partners have the potential for jointly maximizing their outcomes. If they both decide to talk politics they will be equally rewarding to each other. Otherwise they will only gain at the other's expense, and not gain very much at that. We would predict that those two would usually end up talking politics rather than telling jokes. They have a potentially compatible relationship. The couple in figure 3(b) unfortunately can each gain only at the other's expense, whatever course of action they embark on, and since there is no possibility of mutual reward they can only be described as incompatible. We would expect their interactions and their relationship to be unstable and short-lived as they go through each possible combination of behaviours and find them to be unrewarding for one of them.

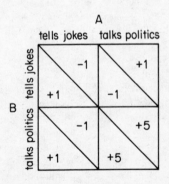

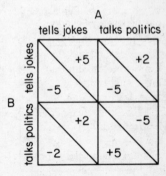

Figure 3(a) A potentially compatible relationship

Figure 3(b) A potentially incompatible relationship

Not only can we represent incompatibility clearly in this manner, but we can also represent inequality and potentially exploitative relationships too. When relationships are unequal it means that one person has potential power over the other who is in fact dependent on them. In terms of the analysis here it means that A is more powerful than B, if he can affect B's outcomes more than B can affect A's outcomes. He can then use this potential to extract from B behaviour or any other resource that he wants. The situation is represented in figure 4. Here A is a pupil and B a teacher. If we compare the outcomes for A when B takes one course of action rather than another we find that it makes very little difference (the difference is +3 versus +2 and +1 versus +1). On the other hand what A does makes a lot more difference to B (the difference is 0 versus +4 and 0 versus +3). As it stands the situation is one only of potential power. However, A might be able to exploit the situation in such a way that he or she can withhold rewarding behaviour until the teacher does something that A does want. Unfortunately, however, as soon as A wants something that the teacher can offer, the power potential is equalized. This means that as soon as one party wishes to use their potential power by getting something they want, their want moves towards destroying the power base. In their recent work Thibault and Kelley (1978) have explored this and other forms of the tendency in relationships towards equalizing power and therefore towards interdependency, which they argue is a strong force.

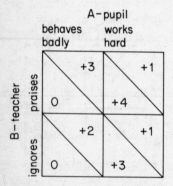

Figure 4 A teacher–pupil relationship

As their recent work shows, the matrices which can characterize different human transactions are very numerous, but the two key features of any matrix are (1) whether or not it includes one cell, or more than one cell, in which both parties can equally maximize their outcomes, and (2) the size of the difference in outcomes for any party as a result of the other's actions.

The model is presented here in a most skeletal form, and the reader who wishes to explore more of its possibilities is directed towards Thibault and Kelley (1978) and Gergen *et al.* (1980). The outcome analysis presented there is nevertheless somewhat academic because it remains hypothetical. However, it provides an invaluable tool for analysing features of one's relationships in a systematic way.

But what, from empirical research, do we know to be well interpreted within this framework? First, what do we know of the factors that people find rewarding in each other? It is possible in terms of exchange theory to think about this in terms of both rewards and costs. For example people may well enter into transactions with others where the rewards are not necessarily particularly high but the costs are very low, and therefore the transaction is profitable. This might be one explanation of the finding that people like others who are situated in close proximity to them. Festinger *et al.* (1950), in the study discussed in chapter 3, found that neighbours who were easily accessible for interaction were preferred to those who were not, that is, rewards value being equal, the low costs of available neighbours led to liking. In fact the same authors found that if people who lived at a distance *were* nominated as friends they tended to be more liked on other criteria, that is they had to be that much more rewarding to offset the costs of going to see them. The same interpretation could be placed on the widespread finding that we prefer people who are similar to us in beliefs, values and attitudes (Kandel, 1978). Again, to be faced with someone whose understanding of the world around them is markedly different from our own is costly since so little can be taken for granted and so much more has to be debated and possibly argued about during the relationship. Unless there is some important other source of reward, then the costs are going to make the relationship uneconomic. With a similar other the costs are kept low by our not having to debate basic issues all the time.

Some characteristics of people which are widely valued seem to be rewarding in themselves, independently of the costs. For example physical attractiveness, particularly in women, is a widely valued resource. Men who are simply *seen* with physically attractive women gain in value from spectators, who judge them to be more successful and likeable, which clearly bestows a resource on them (Bar-Tal and Saxe, 1976a). Intelligence is also generally valued in our culture, in both sexes (Solomon and Saxe, 1977). We like people with positive traits of all sorts, people who are reasonably happy, outgoing, friendly, and so forth. Our preferences are quite clear. We would like to invest our resources in those who are attractive, intelligent, successful, well-adjusted, happy and outgoing. Whether we manage to restrict ourselves, however, to this desirable end of the human continuum depends, according to exchange theory, on what we have to offer.

Take physical attractiveness as an example. Studies of both couples (Murstein, 1972) and of friends of the same sex (Cash and Derlega, 1978) show that we end up in relationships with others who are similar to us in generally judged physical attractiveness. Not only that, when we have a chance to choose others our choices are predicted both by how attractive the other is and by how likely they are to choose us (Shanteau and Nagy, 1976). The lay person seems to share the social-exchange theorist's view, namely that we opt for the possible and available in our relationships.

Relationships are not static in terms of the exchange of rewards and costs. In the early stages of acquaintanceship people both invest relatively little and incur relatively few costs and get few rewards. The early stages are occupied with the estimation process in which people are concerned with looking for signs of rewards which might become available in the future and which show signs of increasing, and this becomes an important factor in the decision to continue with an investment (Levinger and Huessmann, 1980). Clearly, during this stage it is important to keep one's investments and costs low. A relationship which continues beyond this point will go through stages in which there is an increase in mutual interest or interdependence. The far end of this process is exemplified by the couple 'in love' who then become marriage partners, in which their outcomes are mutually compatible and highly interdependent (Rands and Levinger, 1979).

Interestingly, reported rewards from established relationships appear to diminish over time, and one of the reasons for this is likely to be the individual's habituation to a particular level and type of reward (Swenson, 1978) which can be provided by one partner over a long period of time.

A model of human behaviour may be highly plausible and make the interpretation of our experiences and research findings intelligible. Nevertheless we have always to consider the limits of its applicability. What are the limitations of the social-exchange model? The model is limited wherever the basic assumptions do not hold – for example, where people have limited choices in relationships because of the existence of strong supra-personal habits and customs or strong values, or because of lack of mobility through handicap, indeed any constraint on choice. In many parts of the world, for example, marriage is not a matter which involves the choice of the couple at all; it is organized according to other criteria for the benefit of wider kin groups. Relationships generally may be strongly constrained by the kinship system, with rights and obligations which define who may have relationships with whom and to what level of exchange. *We* live in a consumer, capitalistic society both in terms of the material world and in terms of the social and interpersonal world. Here the model has plausibility. Yet even we recognize constraints which supersede idiosyncratic and personal choice. One of these constraints is the generalized belief in the importance of equity in human relationships. The belief in equity in human relationships concerns the prescription that we ought to benefit according to our investments and that the benefits that others gain should be similarly in accordance with their investments, and, in the end ratio between investment and rewards, people should be on a par. If we extract more from a relationship than we put into it we should feel uncomfortable and guilty, and if we put in more than we get out we should feel angry (all this is relative to the partners involved). Thibault and Kelley argue that relationships tend towards equity anyway, but others have argued that we have in addition a strong value or implicit rule system that demands that equity should appear to prevail.

There is a certain amount of research which suggests that with couples, for example, where a partner felt there to be inequity there was less satisfaction with the relationship (Walster *et al.* 1978). The investment, in this study, was usually defined by the partners themselves and concerned anything they felt was contributed by the marriage partner like appearance, help, money-earning capacity, emotional support and companionship. Although there may be a strong tendency towards equity in relationships, as in other aspects of social exchange, it is technically difficult to specify or quantify these relationships between investments and outcomes. A person may, for example, be in a relationship which from the outsider's point of view appears inequitable. However, the parties concerned may not attach the same values to the negative investments as the outsider does. For example much of the input from women into marriage and family life has traditionally been taken for granted, that is accorded a lower value than such investments as earning the family income or fixing the car.

Much social change is based on the efforts of some parties to re-evaluate the investments of groups which are seen to be exploited by being trapped in inequitable relationships. Thus much of the feminist movement is concerned with gaining a revaluation of women's contributions in many fields, so that where inequity *is* pertaining it will be *seen* to be pertaining. We see the same process at work in the field of wage-bargaining. Most disputes concern the relationships between investments, in the form of danger, disagreeable working conditions, unsocial hours, qualifications, responsibility, etc., and outputs, in the form of wages. The frequent failure to reach agreement on what constitutes an equitable solution is due to the fact that forces for change begin to dispute the relative value of investments. For example it might be disputed now that university graduates' inputs in the form of their longer years of education should be counted as an investment, or that white-collar workers should enjoy fringe benefits. The evaluation of investments both in society and interpersonally are a potent force for revolutions at both levels.

How would such an analysis assist us in exerting more control over our relationships? Let us go back to a basic statement about the effects of reward on human behaviour. The most basic statement ever made about this was that a reward was anything that increased the probability of behaviour (Skinner, 1953). This suggests that the problem of finding out which rewards control behaviour is a pragmatic one. It suggests that first we identify the actual piece of behaviour that we are seeking to explain. Let us imagine as an example that a teacher wants to find out why a pupil keeps on dropping all the books and papers from the desk and creating a great disturbance. Actually the teacher wants the pupil to stop doing this and to finish the project that has been given out. Rather like Kelley's lay psychologist, the teacher will look for co-variation between the annoying behaviour and its results. The teacher may find that one frequent outcome of the fracas is that several other children laugh. This can be tested out by surreptitiously removing the other children, or surreptitiously persuading them to ignore the offending behaviour, and examining the rate at which the behaviour declines, just as a psychologist might watch the decline in the bar-pressing behaviour of a rat in a Skinner box as its behaviour failed to produce pellets of food. There are many apocryphal stories of how people have managed unobtrusively to get others to begin all their sentences with 'I' or 'personally speaking' simply by giving them little nods of approval every time they did so, or to keep lecturers in one corner of the lecture room by smiling at them every time they moved in the desired direction. Both at the level of interaction and at the level of more long-term transactions we should be watching for those events which have some shaping effect on others.

We can analyse our own sources of reward in the same way. Indeed we can construct for ourselves hypothetical outcome matrices to try to make explicit certain features of our relationships with other people according to the criteria mentioned earlier in the chapter. Such an exercise could focus our attention more clearly on what were the real costs and rewards of particular transactions, particularly recurring ones, and what were the real costs and rewards to the other. Such an analysis would force us out of some of the unthinking routines we get into and allow us the chance of a little more choice and control in our relationships.

9

The management of social interaction and social relationships

Talk and action are the visible, front-line elements of daily encounters. Behind this front line lie the supply lines of attitudes, values, resources and beliefs, and feelings about ourselves and about others. Helping people to improve their encounters and relationships with others requires attention, both to the front lines but also to the supply lines. Although training programmes for managing social interaction have focused to a large extent on behaviour, we shall also be concerned here with programmes for the analysis and modification of feelings and beliefs. Let us begin by providing some perspective for social-skills training within the broader context of general programmes for personal change.

Two approaches to personal change

Aside from drug and other physical interventions, approaches to personal change are really of two types – action therapies and insight therapies. Insight therapies consist of therapists and clients talking about the client's situations and relationships, both present and past. Present problems are related to each other and to past events, and the therapist interprets the material in terms of certain motivational patterns or themes. The interpretive frameworks vary according to the therapist's orientations; Freud, Jung, Klein, Perls and others have provided theoretical frameworks for understanding the long-term conduct of individuals. Many of these locate the origins of present problems in early childhood, and increasing the awareness of these origins is part of the therapeutic process. In some insight therapies the client's, as opposed to the therapist's, interpretation of underlying themes guides the therapeutic process (as for example in the client-centred therapy of Carl Rogers). The basic assumptions behind insight therapies are as follows: that inadequate or problematic social behaviour is caused by underlying fears and conflicts, that is the manifest symptoms of present problems are caused by latent emotional processes; that changing behaviour will not be successful without modifying the latent process; that the specialized talk that takes place between clients and therapists and the 'insights' that ensue (and in some cases the emotional processes which take place between the two of them) are both the necessary and sufficient conditions for clients to realize the changes they want in their lives.

One of the main problems with the approaches to personal change through interpretation and insight is that the patterns and themes which the therapist (or for that matter the client) 'sees' may only exist inside their heads (Nisbett and Ross, 1980). As we learned in chapter 6, much of what we see is determined not so much by what may or may not be there, but by our prior *beliefs* about what is there. Thus there is always the possibility that clients emerge with new sets of lenses through which to view their own conduct and circumstances, but with both the latter substantially unchanged. This problem may be partly answered if we find ways to assess and evaluate different approaches, but the technical problems of doing so are very great indeed.

Action therapies on the other hand are aimed at directly changing clients' behaviours, or rather, helping clients to change their own behaviours, because as we saw earlier there has been a shift in emphasis towards self-management. One of the reasons for this shift in focus has been the recognition that whatever is learned or changed in a consulting room has to be applied in a variety of situations in the outside world, and from a practical point of view only the clients will encounter and manage those situations. Another reason has been the recognition, as we saw in chapter 7, that a sense of control over one's own actions and outcomes is in itself a component of well-being. Self-management techniques are aimed at the client's realization of that control.

Social-skills training is concerned with modifying actual behaviour with others. However, not all action therapies are concerned simply with changing behaviour. They are often aimed also at actually changing what clients are doing, thinking and feeling at the present time. But the problems described are focused on directly as they are presented, rather than interpreted in terms of some other underlying process. Thus clients may be taught techniques for modifying their physiological responses of fear, for example by learning techniques of progressive relaxation to those events which evoke fear. Or they may be taught to monitor particular patterns of thought which accompany depression or anxiety and to modify them, criticize them and substitute other arguments for them.

Who are the clients?

In the past twenty years or so there has been a considerable expansion in the population of people who have voluntarily become involved with techniques for personal change. The most obvious recipients of personal-change therapy programmes are those admitted to psychiatric clinics with severe problems which cripple them both socially and occupationally. In addition to these, however, many become involved for professional reasons because their jobs involve the management of other people – teachers, interviewers for selection and research, psychotherapists themselves, managers, and many others. The distinctions between practitioner and client have in this respect become less sharp. However, it should be remembered that there are people whose social competence is very severely impaired and this is quite apparent simply from observing them in routine situations. Such people can be distinguished easily from the rest of the clinical population with general emotional problems (Trower *et al.*, 1974) in that their social behaviour is lacking in expressiveness and is leaden and unresponsive, and their conversation is sparse and monotonous. Programmes concerned with developing more adequate *behaviour* are particularly relevant to such clients.

Social conduct and values

Except when we are dealing with clients with gross deficits in their social behaviour, and who are extremely isolated on that account, many of the goals of personal change are dependent on particular values being adopted. How we should conduct ourselves with others, the bases of our relationships with others, the relative importance that we attach to our own well-being as opposed to that of others, are questions of value in which professional psychologists have no particular or greater authority than anyone else.

If we look at some of the goals implicit in programmes for increasing social effectiveness we often come across the following: enhancing one's capacity to act autonomously and as individuals rather than collectively (or some would say collusively); asserting oneself rather than being submissive; expressing one's feelings openly instead of hiding them; and so forth. None of these values are written up in the sky to be observed for all time. They are relative to our own culture and moment in history. As psychologists we often imagine that certain patterns of behaviour are synonymous with mental health. We must remember that they are so only to the extent that it is *usually* more adaptive to behave in ways which are generally valued in society than in ways that are not.

Values enter into programmes of change in so far as they are informing clients' behaviours without the latter being quite aware of their doing so. For example some people walk around with hidden agendas in their heads that tell them that they must comply with the wishes of others or that their behaviour ought to be consistent all the time. Failure to recognize such hidden agendas can inhibit people's progress to their other personal goals.

Values are supply lines, but even more important are the ideas and feelings we entertain about ourselves and others. We examined in chapter 7 some varieties of self-awareness that have relevance for our behaviour and relationships with other people, and in chapter 6 some of the processes we bring to bear on

143

understanding other people, which have similar relevance. In the next section we will consider ways in which both may be investigated and modified in the context of therapeutic intervention.

Modifying beliefs about oneself

Beliefs about emotional states

Our general social effectiveness, and certainly our relationships with other people, are often undermined by feelings we find unable to control, feelings of fear and anxiety, anger and depression. Many of us believe that emotional states lie outside the individual's control. We often believe that we can and should control the *expression* of emotions, but we more rarely believe that we can control their actual occurrence. In chapter 7 it was pointed out that emotional experience is a product of three interacting factors: internal physiological arousal; the interpretation of environmental events; and our own recurring thoughts. Some recent developments in self-management techniques have been based on the assumption that people can intervene in any or all of these components. Anxiety and depression can have a great impact on social behaviour, and since programmes for dealing with both have been well-developed let us use these as examples of the self-management of emotional states.

Take the case of anxiety. People may experience anxiety in all kinds of situations, including anxiety about task-achievement, as in examinations, anxiety about asserting oneself in company, and anxiety about one's response to potentially painful medical interventions. Extreme anxiety can become phobic, and this is found with respect to, for example, closed spaces (claustrophobia), open spaces (agoraphobia) and creatures like moths, snakes and spiders. Whatever the anxiety-evoking situation, the experience of anxiety has certain invariable components. One component is physiological – sweating palms, butterfly stomach, increased heart rate, tremors and dry mouth. Another component is attentional, that is being unable to concentrate on the elements of the task or behaviour in hand and concentrating only on fearful thoughts about the situation. This is particularly obvious in situations like examinations or social occasions where one attends not to the actual performance but to the consequences of not performing well, or one experiences attention-moving from one irrelevant stimulus to another. Another is simply the unpleasant thoughts and predictions surrounding the frightening situation. Anxiety also produces failure of memory, both in retrieving and in storing new material. And it leads to poorer performance and rigid, inflexible approaches to a problem.

Self-management techniques provide clients with strategies for changing all these components. For example, deep relaxation, which is achieved only by active concentration, involves regulating the breathing and progressive muscle relaxation, and is incompatible with the physiological symptoms of anxiety. Clients can be taught to use some neutral image as a cue to producing this relaxed state. Then they can be taught immediately to identify the somatic components of anxiety and to substitute the relaxed state. They can be asked to imagine a hierarchy of situations ranging from the mildly to the severely stressful and to practise relaxation in each increasingly stressful situation. Having learned the basic skills, clients can then practice them *in vivo*. They will learn the characteristics of the situation which initiate physiological anxiety, and use relaxation techniques as soon as the somatic symptoms occur and before they are beyond control. Over a period of time they will test out this technique in increasingly stressful situations as they occur in the normal context. However, because anxiety occurs in response not so much to the objective features of situations but to one's appraisal of them, this appraisal too has to become the focus of change.

This aspect of self-management involves therapists and clients in examining in detail the ideas, beliefs and expectations clients have about certain situations. These ideas are conceptualized as self-statements that arouse anxiety and therefore they need to be neutralized. One term for this process is 'systematic rational restructuring,' which derives from the rational-emotive therapy of Albert Ellis (1962). Beliefs which arouse and support states of anxiety, for example, usually involve the following: failure to appreciate the real probability of catastrophic events, as in fears about flying; unrealistic, but unacknowledged, expectations about the outcomes of some action, such as not accepting the fact that one is unlikely to get a first-class degree; false beliefs that one could not cope with some eventuality at all, as opposed to recognizing that it would be unpleasant, but not catastrophic;

beliefs that other people's approval is absolutely necessary for one's survival, rather than simply a pleasant state. The joint tasks of therapists and clients are identifying these underlying beliefs and assumptions, specifying them in terms of actual statements and finding counter-beliefs as antidotes. The client's self-management tasks are then to monitor their thought processes and actively practise the more positive statements, again *in vivo*, when the situations crop up. The performance component involves setting small, realizable goals for coping with the task that produces anxiety, identifying the behaviours which will lead to the goal and acknowledging the point when one achieves them (Deffenbacher and Suinn, 1982).

We see a similar programme of self-management in depression. Clinically depressed individuals show a number of characteristics which include apathy, changes in eating habits, loss of interest in previously enjoyed activities and people, and, above all, negative thoughts about themselves, their achievements and their prospects, the latter showing as a sense of helplessness and incapacity to change any feature of their life. Not surprisingly, this is all accompanied by emotions of sadness and, at worst, despair. The syndrome itself is variously accompanied by changes in brain chemistry, which in themselves may then play an important role in the maintenance of depressive states.

Self-management techniques in depression are focused on changing negative thought processes. There is evidence that depressed people show distortions in the way in which they monitor events (Hughes *et al.*, 1982). They attend to and remember negative events more than positive events, in particular those which have a bearing on self-esteem. Their poor sense of their own value is maintained by distorted attributional processes, in which they attribute success to external, often chance, factors and failure to internal causes like lack of ability or effort or both (Beck, 1972). They set standards of achievement for themselves which are unrealistic, so that failure or at least inadequacy are guaranteed (Hughes *et al.*, 1982). All these negative cognitive processes feed self-statements that rarely allow depressed individuals to give themselves any rewards, and only allow themselves continual self-punishment.

A basis for self-management therapy is getting clients to accept the proposition that mood is a function of thoughts and behaviour, as much as the other way round (which is what most depressives believe). Therefore the basis for improving mood has to be changes in thoughts and behaviours. Clients are asked to keep a detailed diary of all the events, large and small, positive and negative, that occur over a period of a few days, as well as the more infrequently occurring ones that have happened over a longer time span. This allows both clients and therapists to examine the real frequencies of different types of event (it will have been suggested to clients previously that they have distorted perceptions of these frequencies). Then they are asked to make a chart showing the relationship between mood changes and events, in order properly to identify the ones most significant for mood changes (recall the study in chapter 7, p. 116). This means that clients can begin to intervene in their monitoring processes, and move from their depressing theories to actual data, like proper scientists.

The next focus of attention will be the relationship between actions and outcomes. Again a careful record is to be kept of the actual outcomes of actions, both in the short term and the long term. Furthermore, depressed people need to examine more objectively the causes of successes and failures, and in particular to pay more attention to situational factors in failure. In this context it is also important to look at some underlying assumptions about competence. For example, Ellis (1962) points out that many people harbour the belief that they have to be extremely competent in *all* domains of activity *all* the time in order to be considered worthwhile. It is impossible to be successful all the time; one has to concentrate one's efforts on those activities over which one has real control and not waste energy on the other sort. And concentrating on processes rather than results is psychologically much more rewarding anyway. In the light of these considerations, clients are asked to set themselves realizable goals; to concentrate on increasing positive behaviours, rather than on getting rid of negative behaviours; to concentrate on things which are frequent, rather than rare, that are under the control of self rather than that of others; and to break down goals into smaller, more attainable sub-goals.

All this is practised outside the clinic, *in vivo*, as homework, and careful records are kept of the results in order to discuss progress and the next steps with the therapist. Finally clients are taught about reward and punishment and their effects on behaviour.

They are asked to list things with which they can reward themselves for successful completion of all the activities listed here. Some of these rewards may be extrinsic, like treats or favoured activities, but more important are the intrinsic ones of using positive self-statements, such as recognizing one's achievements and attributing them to one's own characteristics instead of external factors. All of these strategies must increase clients' sense of control over their own feelings, thus breaking the cycle of apathy and helplessness. If enhanced control over feelings leads to changes in behaviour, and these in turn lead to changes in other people's responses, then clients are on the road to positive self-fulfilling prophecies instead of negative ones.

Beliefs about self as agent

We have already touched on this issue in the foregoing discussion, but some general points need to be emphasized. Often people do not achieve what they want socially because they are passive and allow others to determine the occasions of interaction and the course which the interaction will take. All the principles discussed in the previous section are applicable to the process of interacting with others. People must *do* something in order to change their encounters and relationships, but they won't do so unless they believe that as agents they can be effective. It is important for clients first to be aware of the extent to which they believe themselves to be pawns or agents, and secondly to select areas of social behaviour in their lives where an initiative would most likely produce a direct and positive outcome, since that is the first step towards modifying the beliefs that support passivity. It is equally important to recognize those areas over which one can have very little control, like getting into romantic relationships with people who are already happily engaged elsewhere, or trying to get approval from people who always criticize everyone, because, conversely, acting on an unyielding social environment can only produce helplessness.

Self-esteem and beliefs about one's own value

Beliefs about self can result in self-fulfilling prophecies. If our valuation of ourselves is generally low, that is if we have low self-esteem, then we are likely to act in ways which force others to confirm this evaluation. How might people raise their estimation of themselves? Self-esteem can be considered as the discrepancy between how one would like to be in any particular dimension and how one sees oneself to be. Our views of how we ought to be are constructed out of comparisons with other people. If one chooses as reference points others who seem particularly exalted, this is one way to continue with low self-esteem, just as using Wimbledon champions as standards for evaluating one's tennis-playing would be disheartening and self-punitive. We have already touched on ways in which such beliefs about self are implicated in depression and the techniques for modifying them. The exposure of unnecessarily high expectations about self is one of these. There is another way in which low self-esteem can be produced and exacerbated, and that is through self-consciousness or, as it was called in chapter 7, objective self-awareness. Awareness of self brings about awareness of one's shortcomings. The detached and active monitoring processes described in the earlier section on self-management techniques may have as a side effect a lessening of objective self-awareness and, with that, poor self-evaluation. Behind the issue of self-esteem is the fact that one's absolute value in any dimension is very hard to assess, that one may have to rely on setting one's own standards, and that from a social point of view, veridical or not, high self-esteem has more positive social consequences than has low self-esteem. The problem of self-consciousness brings us to another important belief about self.

Self-consciousness and being 'authentic'

Our experience of ourselves, as we saw in chapter 7, includes a distinction between a private self, to which no one need have access without permission, and the public self which we choose to present. A large discrepancy between the two can lead to crises of sincerity since we often view the private self as the more authentic. In social-skills-training programmes in which people are asked to play roles or to practise social routines in order to create a good impression, this kind of self-consciousness can be an inhibitor. Self-consciousness declines with practice, as any stage actor will tell any life actor, even though getting someone started on these routines is a problem for social-skills trainers. It is worth considering beliefs, however, which may make the problem of sincerity worse. One widely held belief, is that one has one *real* self, and that the *real*, authentic self is the one that is private and unseen by others. The validity of such a belief is a matter for philosophical debate which the clients can better take up outside clinics and hospitals. What has to be stressed is that one may give different impressions of oneself at different times and one has a right to be variable, that is one may legitimately place as much confidence in any particular social self or person that one brings to a situation as one may in one's private, hidden self.

Beliefs about other people

The impressions that we form of other people and the motives that we ascribe to them have a direct bearing on how we behave with them. If we believe that someone is critical of us, we will behave defensively; if we believe that someone is trying to please us, we will act positively. In chapter 6 we saw a number of potential biases in the way in which we form judgements of others. Many of these derive from basing our judgements on too little information from a person and relying too much on rarely examined theories of what they are like. Let us remind ourselves of some examples.

On the basis of a person's category membership – ethnic, occupational age, physical type or any other – we can activate a schema or stereotype about that person's character which biases our attention towards information confirming the stereotype and makes us relatively insensitive to information which does not accord with it. In order to trace the degree to which our behaviour towards another is based on such a process, we need to reconstruct and examine the evidence for beliefs we have about others which are based on category membership, and to search for information which does not confirm those beliefs. Both processes result in delaying judgement about others as well as heightened attention to their actual behaviour.

Similarly we have seen that we pay disproportionate weight to early impressions, especially if they are negative. Again, order effects can be disrupted by deliberately paying attention to later information and by acknowledging any judgements that have been made on the basis of first impressions.

The fundamental attribution error is that of paying too little attention to the extent to which situational factors constrain behaviour, and locating too many causes in other people's intentions and characters, thus allowing us to form premature judgements of their enduring dispositions. This is particularly likely if their behaviour is thought to be directed specifically towards us and if their behaviour has strong consequences. Again, simply considering the role of external factors in shaping a person's conduct will delay judgement and make a considered response a possibility. Over-reaction to the outcomes of other people's behaviour can short-circuit our search for all causal factors. Of course, making judgements of responsibility and according blame is one way in which we think to mitigate the pain of painful events. Whether that strategy succeeds or fails, it impedes the search for the real nature of the situation.

From the point of view of interpersonal behaviour, one of the most important pieces of information about others is their beliefs about and attitudes towards us. Since there are many social constraints on airing directly one's opinions of others, it is rare that our perceptions of others' perceptions are based on any very solid information. It is with respect to these processes that small groups as a context for personal change are so productive, since they provide a 'cultural island' where usual constraints on behaviour are lifted (even if new ones are imposed!). In encounter groups or other 'experiential' groups, strangers are bought together for the sole purpose of examining their reactions to one another and the feelings that arise in this relatively unstructured context.

These situations provide the ideal material for exploring one's perception of others and their perceptions of oneself, and to test them against the different views of other group members. Whether one considers stereotypes, first impressions, others' perceptions of self or attributional biases, the group provides a context for the corrective examination of one's beliefs about others and their beliefs about self, which dyadic therapy does not. These explorations may provide the necessary conditions for seeing the perspectives of others in role-taking. The latter in turn forms part of any strategy for resolving interpersonal conflicts and generating skills for dealing with difficult interpersonal situations.

Understanding outcome structures in exchange

Finally we usually need to be more aware of what benefits we accrue from our actions, and what benefits others around us are accumulating from our joint transactions. Such an analysis does not entail that we commit ourselves entirely to the costs–benefits view of human life presented in chapter 8, only that we recognize that costs and benefits play some role and that looking for the outcome structures in our dealings with others may make sense of patterns of interaction that have become established, and direct our attention towards possibilities for change. We need to look realistically at what rewards we have to offer and to sensitize ourselves to what we are finding rewarding. Only observation over time can show what these are.

Language skills as a resource

The most important skills that we can acquire for managing social interaction are linguistic ones. Our knowledge of the phonemic and morphemic features of our own language is automatic, and our knowledge of the syntactic rules which link propositions together is largely automatic, but variously extensive. It has often been assumed by psychologists who study language that people automatically reach a standard level of syntactic competence in their first language. However, surveys of literacy suggest that this may not be automatic at all. At the heart of general educational curricula should be programmes which help people to explore the linguistic knowledge they implicitly hold and to examine ways of both extending it and putting it to more use, much as one would with pupils learning a foreign language to a high level of competence. Beyond the myriad ways we have for constructing sentences there are the knowledge and skills involved in planning different types of discourse: instructions and specifications have to be organized in terms of what the listener already knows, and in terms of what anyone would need to know to deal with each item in a set of instructions; the art of telling stories, whether true or fictional, is an infinite one, involving an appreciation of dramatic structure, imagery, adequate and telling detail, as opposed to a total recall of dull and unnecessary detail, keeping a proper balance between background information or details about the setting, and the events critical to the plot.

Central to all this is the understanding of meaning, both denotative meaning and connotative meaning, that is the affective power words can have over other people, to which attention was drawn in chapter 4. The analysis of literary texts, advertisements, propaganda and the mass media is a prerequisite of understanding the use of language for social purposes, and again should be part of general education, and furthermore a continuing source of awareness throughout one's life since the tools of language are changing all the time. From this analysis one can derive exercises to develop verbal skills for use in interaction. We see ways of developing people's verbal skills in a structured manner in programmes for teaching English as a second language. It is beyond the scope of this text to develop a programme for linguistic skills as part of social-skills training. Suffice to say that it is a crucial and, so far, largely neglected component of such training.

Social interaction as a skilled performance

The social-skills model

Throughout this book reference has been made to social-skills training and the idea of social interaction as a skilled performance. What justification is there for talking about social interaction in this way? We do so because it is possible to consider it as involving many of the components involved in other skills. First there is a hierarchy of sub-skills which with practice become increasingly autonomous and outside the awareness of the actor. In playing tennis, the shifts of weight from one foot to another, the positioning of the feet, the sweep of the arm, the tossing up of the ball and the final strike have to be acquired by the learner, individually and consciously; in the skilled player they become the whole sweep of movement which constitutes the service. Similarly in social interaction the positioning and orientation of the body, the eyebrow movement, the various facial grimaces which signal 'pleasure', 'surprise' and the launching of the first topic seem to the unskilled separate and awkward moves. In the skilled performer, however, they become the smooth sequence of behaviour which is involved in the charming greeting.

Secondly there is the fact that such sequences of action are under the continuous control of feedback. The tennis player adjusts position to adapt to the speed of the ball descending in service and to the position of the other player. If any of these or other variables change, the player will take corrective action, again without awareness. Similarly, if one prepares to greet someone who, before one speaks, yells, 'Hi, I've got to dash for the bus', or returns one's look with an expression of incomprehension, one will, if a skilled actor, short-circuit the prepared greeting without perhaps even being aware of doing so. Seen in this way it is useful to consider social interaction as a form of skill and to design programmes for its development according to the principles found effective in the development of other, non-social skills. These are, in particular, the principles of regular practice, of continual feedback on progress, of isolating the sub-skills and practising them as well as synthesizing them into the larger hierarchies and practising those. This model has provided a basis for programmes for improving social effectiveness, as the following examples will show.

Some skill elements

In chapter 2 we saw that many sequences of interaction are apparently rule-following since they seem so predictable in their formats. Greetings, farewells, the structure of many conversations in terms of adjacent pairs of items, like question–answer, complaint–commiseration, statement–agreement/disagreement. These sequences are below the awareness of most of us because they do not cause us any trouble. Indeed it is necessary to read a book on social psychology in order to become aware of this hidden structure of everyday life. For some, very shy people, however, these elements are no more automated than staying on a bicycle is for a non-cyclist. Failure to perform such lower-order skills clearly impedes the development of higher-order ones like dating and winning arguments or indeed making friends at all. Training in social skills is based, as we said before, on action therapy, that is that clients have to act differently in some way in order for change to occur, and it has to include self-management since ultimately only clients can use their improved skills in the real-life situations where they actually need them.

Professionals may, from their interviews with clients, identify part of the problem as failure to master the basic automatic skills of interaction. Clients then need two things: first an awareness of the common, usually unnoticed sequences of social interaction; and secondly some feedback about where their behaviour omits or distorts such sequences. To meet the first of these needs, clients, like other social scientists, can examine sequences of interaction. These can be recorded on film, described in books like this one, observed *in vivo* at the suggestion of therapists to keep detailed accounts of interaction in natural settings, or simply described and modelled by therapists. Clients will also benefit from observing material which shows these sequences being mismanaged by others. They should by then have caught up with therapists in being able to describe quite accurately these common elements.

Clients also need information about their own typical performances. Like most learning, seeing is a more effective means than hearing about. One of the reasons why we all fail to achieve ideal standards of social performance is that we never have the chance to observe our own behaviour from the perspective of an observer. A crucial element in social-skills training is the provision of that perspective, usually through some kind of hardware like video screening, on a sample of the client's social performance. Preferably this would be obtained unobtrusively, that is without the client's awareness, in order that it be a typical sample. Thus a client might be televised while speaking in a group of other clients or during the initial interview with therapists. Often it is not possible to disguise this kind of observation and one simply hopes that awareness of the recording equipment will diminish after a short while. When clients receive this feedback they need to observe it with the same objectivity and precision as therapists should, that is not in terms of evaluation or criticism, but in terms of what actually happens. Armed with this information, clients may be in a position to formulate their own diagnosis and start to plan a programme for change. Then comes the difficult part. At some point clients have not only to learn but to practise, and to practise until actual conversational sequences are automatic. The difficulty lies in the fact that this kind of exercise can induce extreme self-consciousness in people who are probably most vulnerable to it and least equipped to deal with it. A lot here depends on the qualities of the therapists. Therapists who are themselves unselfconscious about practising social routines and able to show confidence in clients' eventual success will help a lot. Then sheer habituation lessens the effects of self-consciousness, so that routines may have to be practised repeatedly, in the same way as stage actors go through the same sequence many times or the novice learner of a foreign language practises verbal formulae, until they become detached from a sense of self-evaluation (which may well be a critical component for clients anyway).

Here is an example of a greeting routine from the manual for social-skills training developed by Trower *et al.* (1974), in which the therapists and clients role-play a typical greeting sequence, taking it in turns to initiate the sequence:

A [looks, shows recognition, using the 'eyebrow flash' (see chapter 5)]
B [greets] Hello, George.
A How are you? [and/or] How's the work going?
B I'm fine, how are you? [or] I'm fine, got a rush job on at the moment, see you.
A I've just been to. . . . [or] See you later, cheers.

There are many conversational junctures which can be practised in the same way, with respect both to the verbal elements and the non-verbal elements, like smiling.

Many clients fail with habitual sequences because they are too passive to play the equal role which defines a conversation. For example they may never ask questions, which is a standard practice for maintaining a conversation. One exercise then might be to try out sequences in which they systematically increase the ratio of questions they ask. Similarly, failing to be aware of different types of question, they may not notice questions in which more extended answers would fit and simply reply mono-syllabically; and again the conversation falters both for lack of raw material and because the passivity is interrupting some of the normal assumptions underlying conversations. Similar treatment can be accorded to sequences which terminate conversation (see Schegloff and Sacks' work (1973), described in chapter 2), that is clients may have to practise terminating conversation when they want to, with a variety of partners showing a range of difficulties. The components of terminal sequences involve non-verbal elements as well as verbal strategies, and the former too will have to receive specific attention before being put together.

The other normally automated behaviour which a client may have failed to master, and which again shows strong regularity in any given culture, is the non-verbal behaviour involved in meshing skills. We saw in chapter 4 that normally in conversation the floor passes from one to another via turn-claim signals which involve head nods on the part of the listener and eye signals on the part of the speaker. The topic too passes from one to the other and each has the problem of fading out a topic before introducing a new one. Once again our basic teaching resources are those which make clients aware of the normative nature of many of these devices; of providing them with feedback about their own typical handling of conversations and identifying where these become unsatisfactory; then practising, either in role play with therapists or through group or dyadic situations with other clients which therapists have set up, the conversational junctures where the talk and topic pass from one to another.

Listening

Communication involves sending signals and receiving them. Social-skills training in these aspects can be considered separately. We all fail at times to listen, for certain common reasons. One frequent reason is that we are actually preoccupied with ourselves or something external to the situation. This often happens even while we continue to give off the automatic signals to the other person that indicate listening. Another reason is that we often believe that we know what the other person is saying anyway, that is we guess what they will say but don't check it out by listening to what they actually do say. Consider the following example:

A Would you mind if I opened the window?
B I'm sorry the air is stale in this room.

B has 'heard' 'This room smells', when A had the heat in mind and asked to open the window. Often we listen only partially because we are concerned only with the evaluation of the message, that is whether we like it or agree with it or not, and not to its specific content. Listening is intrinsically difficult because language, as we saw in chapter 4, is based on presuppositions about what others already know and think, and listening reflects these pre-suppositions just as much as speaking does. A lot of the time we are listening to what we think people mean rather than to what they actually say.

Improving one's capacity to listen involves a number of stages. The first one is that of establishing some estimate of how much we actually do listen, and when we don't what the usual reasons for that failure are. A first step in improving listening is that of making it active by intermittently 'reflecting back' to speakers what we think they said or meant. This process both increases one's attention to the talk and also provides some estimate of the accuracy with which one is hearing other people's messages. Not only that; in 'reflecting back', we can also clarify how the other person feels about the subject they are talking about, for example:

A We have put the house up for sale.
B [who had already heard something of the sort] You have really put it up for sale. Was that a sudden decision?

One exercise one can engage in to counteract presuppositions is to keep a mental note of one's actual or implicit response to remarks and to consider the extent to which they were the only relevant ones possible. Moreover, one can equally heighten one's awareness by carrying out this same activity as one listens to others talking amongst themselves. One ideal milieu for these activities is the encounter or sensitivity-training group, where conversational rules are relaxed so that one can pursue the meanings which people are attaching to one another's talk and the validity of those meanings. Improving listening skills really needs more than a dyadic relationship between client and therapist, even though therapists can point out these common failures of the listening process and the reasons for them and assist in the monitoring process which helps clients to identify their specific failures. Once again it is the small-group context which is particularly helpful.

Sensitivity to non-verbal behaviour

We have described the skill of listening attentively and accurately as if we were simply concerned with the verbal content of the message. But the development of sensitivity to other's messages includes understanding the non-verbal elements discussed in chapter 5, which communicate information about others' emotional states and attitudes. One of these non-verbal elements is that of voice qualities, another is facial expression and body movement. Again clients need to be introduced to the idea that there are common expressions of the face which can be identified on quite different types of people. The posed photographs and voices which have been used to assess the average experimental subject's accuracy at detecting emotional states, in the research described in chapter 5, can just as easily be used for training clients in reading and hearing emotional expression. In such training it is particularly important to draw their attention to the components of different facial expressions, for example the role of the mouth, the region around the eyes and eyebrows, and, in the case of voice qualities, to changes in pitch, breathiness, loudness and fading, and so on. In some programmes material can be presented so that only parts of the face are visible. At this stage the clients are simply being given many exemplars of different emotional expressions and analysing their component parts, such as surprised eyes or disgusted mouth. When clients are in groups with others they can also try posing expressions for themselves and allowing others to guess at the expression represented. Then the client can be moved on to actual sequences of expression because, after all, in natural situations peoples' faces and voices are moving and changing, and change may be the significant point. For example the timing of a smile provides a lot of information about its meaning; a smile which fades soon and rapidly after its appearance seems to hide a less than positive feeling. Some expressions are very fleeting and practice is needed in detecting them. Moreover, sequence is important and clients can interpret such sequences as the smile which has followed the impassive stare as opposed to the smile which has followed a frown; the first usually indicates pleasure or surprise or both, but the latter indicates relief. Then the more advanced skill of detecting hidden feelings can be introduced. The cues to 'leakage' are varied and vary between different people. Close acquaintance with someone enables most of us to learn to spot leakage cues. Nevertheless there are some very common ones. The client can be shown those movements which are customarily less under control because unattended to, like movements of feet and legs, or self-stimulation as in scratching, hair twiddling, hand-to-face movements, avoidance, blinking and of course voice qualities. Film and video material can be used and the client asked to attend specifically to the 'hidden' messages in such leakage cues.

Attitudes about situation, the topic and the other person are also detectable from non-verbal cues. Video-taped sequences in which two people are shown in a variety of relationships can be used for decoding interpersonal attitudes as well as transitory states like agreement, disagreement and approval. These are used initially without the sound so that clients won't be distracted from cues in posture, orientation, proximity, congruency and incongruency of posture and orientation, patterns of gaze, all of which provide so much information about the relationships between people, their relative interest in one another, their status differences, and so on. When the sound is available clients can learn to switch attention from the content of what is being said to the hidden cues described.

Decoding, encoding and balance

What about encoding, that is sending messages? As was noted in chapter 4 all our behaviour is informative in some degree, and the main aim of social-skills training is that of giving clients more control over messages which they may be unintentionally sending or failing to send. There are three stages to the process. First there is the analysis of clients' behaviour in interaction. We cannot see our own behaviour and we remain massively unaware a lot of the time of the readings which others make of our behaviour. Feedback which places clients in the position of observers is crucial. For example, people who avoid eye contact to a chronic degree are often completely unaware of this fact until they actually see it. Then there has to be an acquisition of new elements of communication and these have to be practised and their effects observed. Above all clients have to be endlessly pragmatic and endlessly observant about what effects their signals have, because every encounter is slightly different. There can be no formula of behaviour which will always have the same or the desired effect, for one essential element in managing social interaction is that of flexibility.

Although we consider sending and receiving signals as separate elements in training, at a more advanced level the balance between the two needs attention. Some people upset the conversational seesaw because they never really listen to others and they behave independently of another person's response. Others fail because they contribute neither sufficiently nor sufficiently clearly. Many people who are judged to have poor social skills fall into the latter category. Their behaviour is monotonous and unclear because they just don't behave *enough*. The reason, however, why most clients fall into the passive category is because they are more acutely aware of their deficiencies. People who are over-dominant are less likely to refer themselves for help since they are more of a problem to other people than they are to themselves. Again the critical element in displaying imbalances is real feedback spanning a reasonable period of interaction.

The conversation

We are mostly aware of our talk and its effects. The idea of training people in the art of conversation is hardly new and is an important component of education for upper-class people. Language has the dual function of carrying information about the immediate situation and the relationship between the participants, as well as that of carrying the ideational content. Our capacity to utilize the resources of our own language to narrate, explain, instruct, persuade and generally divert cannot be under-estimated, since it probably accounts for more social competence than any other single factor. The skilled talker is a formidable person in any situation. The development of verbal skills is, or should be, a crucial feature of any educational curriculum. As we saw in chapter 4 two major skills are involved in being effective communicators: one is derived from our understanding of the perspective of others, what they need to know and the effects of our behaviour on them; the other is the capacity to choose words and phrases and to structure our discourse adaptively to the listener and to the situation. What are some common problems that people have with conversations? Typically they find it difficult to keep conversations going, or indeed to start them at all, to maintain the interest of others, to elicit the information they may want from other people, or to provide in adequate form the information that others want from them.

Clients often complain that on social occasions they can't think of anything to talk about. But often the problem is not one of a deficit of incidents and observations as conversational material; it is more often clients' failure either to remember them or to regard them as relevant for conversational purposes. For clients who complain of this difficulty one step is simply that of keeping a record over a short period of events and observations which they might like to share with others. Then the problem is that of organizing them as conversational material. One of the first objectives here is that of moving from the general to the specific. If we start with general remarks about something we have done, we can then decide to pursue the topic depending on whether the listeners look interested or not, and if they do, orienting them to what is to follow by putting them in the general picture, which we can follow up with more detail. This aspect of conversation training is particularly well-conducted in groups, since it is quite natural to tell people about events even within the context of a training programme. A second task is that of choosing and planning more personally revealing information, like that of opinions and feelings about things as well as other private information about self. Progress in retailing information goes from the general to the particular, and progress in retailing personally relevant material goes from that evoking a slightly emotive response to that evoking a strongly emotive one. That passage in itself is contingent on listeners' responses, both non-verbal and verbal. For example, in our culture it is less risky to make statement 1 than to make statement 2 to someone whom we do not know very well:

1 We arrived back from Edinburgh last night. It's the first time I've been up there, and I found the people different to what I had expected.
2 We arrived back from Edinburgh last night. I must say I really loathe the Scots.

Self-disclosure

Self-disclosure in interaction, perhaps more than anything else, reveals a matching process to which both parties need to be sensitive. We usually move from topics as personal as home life or job to relationships in general, to family and then to sexual relationships and problems (if we get that far, that is). Each party hazards a personal disclosure and one sign of this move being accepted is that the other party makes a disclosure of a similar order of intimacy. The directness and specificity of the formulation is quite important. One way of introducing a personal area is to make a statement about it in general and to see what happens. For example statement 1 as opposed to 2:

1 Christmas is quite a problem for people who are unattached, don't you think?
2 I can hardly face the thought of Christmas on my own again for the third year running.

Choosing conversational style

We should remember that quite a few people fail in their encounters with others because of an overly inhibited, formal and impersonal style. Only clients and therapists together can spot whether this is the case, and they may be aided in their judgements by video material showing people with very contrasting styles in establishing interpersonal relationships. For the person who uniformly keeps everyone at a distance by a frozen style of talk, the following rules have been suggested (Trower *et al.*, 1974):

Use 'I' rather than 'one', 'they' or 'it'.
Try to bring 'I feel . . .' into the conversation more often.
Use more words which refer directly to the emotion, for example: 'I was absolutely furious', as opposed to: 'It was a real shame that . . .'.
Use facial expressions to match the feeling being expressed verbally.
Use positive forms rather than negative forms: 'I want to', rather than: 'I wouldn't mind . . .'.

Once again the choice and mastering of particular linguistic styles depends partly on understanding the connotative subtleties of language referred to in chapter 4, and is really inseparable from more general linguistic training.

The Olympian heights

In the second part of this chapter we have considered social-skills training in terms of fairly small elements and general processes, relevant to a range of clients, and very much at the level of the average player. We can of course go on to more virtuoso and Olympian tasks like those involved in making amends when one has offended or embarrassed another person; or in resolving very severe conflicts of interest, as is often required between parents and grown-up children; or in holding one's own in conversation with an extremely confident, knowledgeable partner; or in initiating encounters with sexual partners and managing both their acceptances and their rejections; in managing apologies, complaints and arguments with poise. The problems are too diverse and numerous to deal with individually, but there are common elements of training. First, and this is particularly well carried out in groups, there is the listing of critical incidents and situations from real-life experience of clients. Secondly, there is the analysis of actual problems in terms of both parties' perspectives, which often, particularly when focusing on conflict situations, leads on to the strategy of role play, where clients and others not necessarily involved take the parts of the characters involved in the conflict. Thirdly, there is the construction of some actual verbal and behavioural formulae for dealing with the problematic encounters themselves. Fourthly, there is the actual practice either *in vivo*, as a homework assignment, or as a therapeutic exercise. Some excellent and extensive exercises for managing difficult social situations are to be found in *Social Skills and Mental Health* (Trower *et al.*, 1978).

It is at these Olympian heights of social performance that we come to our starting-point – the lay practitioners. We meet them in books, articles and problem-page letters in magazines. These abound with advice and suggestions for handling difficult situations with poise, and indeed charm, and steering relationships into happier fields. It is unlikely that such advice can be easily faulted by any of us. As professionals, however, what we have to offer is precision. We need to be precise about what clients actually do, think and feel. We need to be precise about what they want to change. We need to be precise about whether the changes they do instigate have the desired effects. Above all we want to bring them over to our side and get them to be pragmatic and precise for themselves, effective monitors of and coaches for their *own* social performance. Thus we close on a central theme of this book: that of the close relationship in psychology between scientists and lay persons, and the potential for personal enhancement which can be released when the latter sharpen (with assistance) their own scientific faculties.

Suggestions for further reading

Chapter 1

Giorgi, A. (1970) *Psychology as a Human Science: a Phenomenologically Based Approach*, New York, Harper & Row.

Wegner, D.M. and Vallacher, R. (1977) *Implicit Psychology: an Introduction to Social Cognition*, Oxford, Oxford University Press.

Chapter 2

Brissett, D. (1975) *Life as Theatre: a Dramaturgical Sourcebook*, Hawthorne, NY, Aldine Publishers.

Goffman, E. (1967) *Interaction Ritual: Essays on Face-to-Face Behavior*, New York, Pantheon Books.

Goffman, E. (1968) *Stigma: Notes on the Management of Spoiled Identity*, Harmondsworth, Penguin.

Goffman, E. (1972) *Relations in Public: Microstudies of the Public Order*, Harmondsworth, Penguin.

Chapter 3

Moos, R. (1976) *The Human Context: Environmental Determinants of Behavior*, New York, Wiley.

Chapters 4 and 5

Aaron, W. (ed.) (1979) *Non-verbal Behavior: Applications and Cultural Implications*, New York, Academic Press.

Clark, H. and Clark, E. (1977) *Psychology and Language: An Introduction to Psycholinguistics*, New York, Harcourt Brace Jovanovich.

Chapter 6

Harvey, J. and Smith, W. (1977) *Social Psychology: an Attributional Approach*, St Louis, Mosby.

Nisbett, R. and Ross, L. (1980) *Human Inference: Strategies and Shortcomings*, Englewood Cliffs, NJ, Prentice-Hall.

Chapter 7

Hewitt, J. (1976) *Self and Society: a Symbolic Interactionist Social Psychology*, Newton, Mass., Allyn & Bacon.

Kleinke, C. (1978) *Self-Perception: the Psychology of Personal Awareness*, San Francisco, W.H. Freeman.

Chapter 8

Gergen, K., Greenberg, M. and Willis, R. (eds) (1980) *Social Exchange: Advances in Theory and Research*, New York, Plenum.

Chapter 9

Karoly, P. and Kanfer, F. (1982) *Self-Management and Behaviour Change: from Theory to Practice*, Oxford, Pergamon.

Thoresen, C. and Mahoney, M. (1974) *Self-Control, Power to the Person*, Baltimore, Brookes/Cole.

Trower, P., Bryant, B. and Argyle, M. (1978) *Social Skills and Mental Health*, London, Methuen.

References and name index

The numbers in italics following each entry refer to page numbers in this book.

Altmann, I. (1972) 'Reciprocity of interpersonal exchange'. Paper presented at the 80th annual meeting of the American Psychological Association. *126*

Argyle, M. (1981) 'Rules versus conventions in everyday situations', in M. Argyle, A. Furnham and J.A. Graham *Social Situations*, Cambridge, Cambridge University Press. *29*

Argyle, M. and Dean, J. (1965) 'Eye-contact, distance and affiliation', *Sociometry* 28, 298–304. *76*

Argyle, M., Graham, J.A., Campbell, A. and White, P. (1979) 'The rules of different situations', *New Zealand Psychologist* 8, 13–22. *34*

Athanasiou, R. and Yoshioka, G.A. (1973) 'The spatial character of friendship formation', *Environment and Behaviour* 5, 43–65. *37*

Baker, J. and Crist, J. (1971) 'Teacher expectancies: a review of the literature', in I. Elashoff and R. Snow (eds) *Pygmalion Reconsidered*, Worthington, Ohio, Charles A. Jones. *96*

Ball, D. (1967) 'An abortion clinic ethnography', *Social Problems* 14, 293–301. *28*

Ball, D. (1970) 'The definition of the situation: some theoretical and methodological consequences of taking W.I. Thomas seriously', in J. Douglas (ed.) *Existential Sociology*, New York, Appleton-Century-Crofts. *28*

Barker, R. (1968) *Ecological Psychology: Concepts and Methods for Studying the Environment*, Stanford, California, Stanford University Press. *35*

Bar-Tal, D. and Saxe, L. (1976) 'Perception of similarity and dissimilarity in attractive couples and individuals', *Journal of Personality and Social Psychology* 33, 772–81. *136*

Beck, A. (1972) *Depression: Causes and Treatment*, Philadelphia, University of Philadelphia Press. *146*

Berlyne, D. (1971) *Aesthetics and Psychobiology*, New York, Appleton-Century-Crofts. *44*

Bernstein, B. (1966) 'Elaborated and restricted codes', *Sociological Inquiry* 2: *Explorations in Sociolinguistics*. *60*

Berscheid, E. and Walster, E. (1974) 'Physical attractiveness', in L. Berkowitz (ed.) *Advances in Experimental Social Psychology*, vol. 7, New York, Academic Press, 158–216. *82*

Birdwhistell, R. (1970) *Kinesics and Context*, Philadelphia, University of Philadelphia Press. *66*

Blumstein, P. and Schwartz, P. (1977) 'Bisexuality: some social psychological issues', *Journal of Social Issues* 33 (2), 30–45. *117*

Brehm, J. W. (1966) *Theory of Psychological Reactance*, New York, Academic Press. *104*

Brookes, M. and Kaplan, A. (1972) 'The office environment: space planning and affective behaviour', *Human Factors* 14, 373–91. *38*

Brown, R. (1965) *Social Psychology*, New York, Free Press. *40*

Cappella, J. (1980) 'Turn-by-turn matching and compensation in talk and silence: new methods and new explanations', in H. Giles, P. Robinson and P. Smith (eds) *Language; Social Psychological Perspectives*, Oxford, Pergamon Press. *76*

Cash, T. and Derlega, V. (1978) 'The matching hypothesis: physical attractiveness among same-sexed friends', *Personality and Social Psychology Bulletin* 4, 240–3. *136*

Certier, B. (1970) 'The exchange of self-disclosures in same-sexed and heterosexual groups of strangers', unpublished PhD thesis, Cincinnati, University of Cincinnati. *125*

Clark, H. and Clark, E. (1977) *Psychology and Language: An Introduction to Psycholinguistics*, New York, Harcourt Brace Jovanovich. *55, 167*

Condon, W. and Ogston, W. (1967) 'A segmentation of behaviour', *Journal of Psychiatric Research* 5, 221–35. *68*

Davitz, J. and Davitz, L. (1959) 'The communication of feelings by content-free speech', *Journal of Communication* 9, 6–13. *72*

Deffenbacher, J. and Suinn, R. (1982) 'The self-control of anxiety', in P.

Karoly and F. Kanfer *Self-Management and Behaviour Change: from Theory to Practice*, Oxford, Pergamon Press. *146*

Denzin, N. (1968) 'The self-fulfilling prophecy and patient-therapist interaction', in S. Spitzer and N. Denzin (eds) *The Mental Patient: Studies in the Sociology of Deviance*, New York, McGraw-Hill. *95*

Duncan, B. (1976) 'Differential social perception and attribution of intergroup violence: testing the lower limits of stereotyping blacks', *Journal of Personality and Social Psychology* 34, 590–8. *73–4, 92*

Dutton, D. and Aron, A. (1974) 'Some evidence for heightened sexual attraction under conditions of high anxiety', *Journal of Personality and Social Psychology* 30, 510–17. *113*

Eibl-Eibesfeldt, I. (1975) *Ethology: The Biology of Behavior*, New York, Holt, Rinehart & Winston. *70*

Eibl-Eibesfeldt, I. (in press) Human ethology: concepts and implications for the science of man: the behavioural and brain sciences. *73*

Ekman, P., Friesen, W. and Ellsworth, P. (1972) *Emotion in the Human Face*, New York, Pergamon Press. *70*

Ekman, P., Wallace, V. and Friesen, W. (1969) 'Non-verbal clues to deception', *Psychiatry* 32, 88–106. *71*

Ellis, A. (1962) *Reason and Emotion in Psychotherapy*, Syracuse, NJ, Lyle Stuart. *145, 147*

Ellsworth, P. and Carlsmith, J. (1968) 'The effect of eye-contact and verbal content on effective responses to a dyadic interaction', *Journal of Personality and Social Psychology* 10, 15–20. *75*

Erdelyi, M. (1974) 'A new look at the new look: perceptual defence and vigilance', *Psychological Review* 81, 1–25. *115*

Erikson, E. (1968) *Identity, Youth and Crisis*, New York, Norton. *119*

Erickson, P. (1979) 'Talking down: some cultural sources of miscommunication in interracial interviews', in W. Aaron (ed.) *Nonverbal Behavior: Applications and Cultural Implications*, New York, Academic Press. *78*

Eysenck, H., Arnold, W. and Meili, R. (1972) *Encyclopedia of Psychology*, vol. 1, Herder, West Germany, Search Press. *29*

Feather, N. (1965) 'The relationship of expectation of success to need achievement and test anxiety, *Journal of Psychology* 1, 118–26. *124*

Feather, N. (1966) 'Effect of prior success and failure on expectations of success and subsequent performance', *Journal of Personality and Social Psychology* 3, 287–98. *124*

Fenigstein, A., Scheier, M. and Buss, A. (1975) 'Public and private self-consciousness: assessment and theory', *Journal of Consulting and Clinical Psychology* 43, 522–7. *101, 111*

Ferrare, N. (1962) 'Institutionalization and attitude change in an aged population', unpublished doctoral dissertation, Western Reserve University. *104*

Festinger, L., Schachter, S. and Back, K. (1950) *Social Pressures in Informal Groups: A Study of Human Factors in Housing*, New York, Harper & Row. *135*

Fishman, P. (1979) 'What do couples talk about when they are alone?', in D. Bultorf and E. Epstein (eds) *Women's Language and Style*, Akron, University of Akron Press. *63*

Forgas, J. (1976) 'The perception of social episodes: categorical and dimensional representations in two different social milieus', *Journal of Personality and Social Psychology* 34 (2), 199–209. *30, 33–4*

Furlong, V. (1976) 'Interaction sets in the classroom', in M. Stubbs and S. Delamont (eds) *Explorations in Classroom Observation*, London, Wiley. *62*

Garfinkel, H. (1967) *Studies in Ethnomethodology*, Englewood Cliffs, NJ, Prentice-Hall. *34*

Geer, J., Davison, G. and Gatchel, R. (1970) 'Reduction of stress in humans through non-veridical perceived control of aversive stimulation', *Journal of Personality and Social Psychology* 16, 731–8. *103*

Gergen, K., Greenberg, M. and Willis, R. (eds) (1980) *Social Exchange: Advances in Theory and Research*, New York, Plenum. *135, 167*

Giles, H., Taylor, D. and Bourkis, R. (1973) 'Towards a theory of interpersonal accommodation through language: some Canadian data', *Language in Society* 2, 177–92. *61*

Goethals, G. and Darley, J. (1977) 'Social comparison theory: an attributional approach', in J. Suls and R. Miller (eds) *Social Comparison Processes*, Washington DC, Hemisphere Halstead.

Goffman, E. (1956) 'Embarrassment and social organization', *American Journal of Sociology* LXII, 264–71. *17*

Goffman, E. (1959) *The Presentation of Self in Everyday Life*, New York, Anchor Books. *39*

Goffman, E. (1961) *Encounters*, Indianapolis, Bobbs-Merrill. *29*

Goffman, E. (1963) *Behavior in Public Places: Notes on the Social Organization of Gatherings*, New York, Free Press. *12, 19*

Goffman, E. (1967) *Interaction Ritual: Essays on Face-to-Face Behavior*, New York, Pantheon Books. *17–18, 48, 167*

Goffman, E. (1971) *Relations in Public: Micro-studies of the Public Order*, New York, Basic Books. *6, 8, 11, 13–15, 39–40*

Goldberg, L. (1978) 'Differential attribution of trait-description terms to oneself as compared to well-liked, neutral and disliked others: a psychometric analysis', *Journal of Personality and Social Psychology* 36, 1012–28. *114*

Goodstein, L. and Reinecker, V. (1974) 'Factors affecting self-disclosure: a review of the literature', *Progress in Experimental Personality Research* 7, 49–74. *125*

Gross, E. and Stone, G. (1964) 'Embarrassment and the analysis of role requirements', *American Journal of Sociology* 70, 1–15. *17*

Gumpertz, J., Jupp, T. and Roberts, C. (1979) 'Crosstalk: a study of cross-cultural communication: background material and notes to accompany the BBC film', National Centre for Industrial Language Training. *77*

Halliday, M. (1970) 'Language structure and language function', in J. Lyons (ed.) *New Horizons in Linguistics*, Harmondsworth, Penguin Books. *59*

Harvey, J. Harris, B. and Barnes, R. (1975) 'Actor-observer differences in the perception of responsibility and freedom', *Journal of Personality and Social Psychology* 32, 22–8. *88*

Heider, F. (1958) *The Psychology of Interpersonal Relations*, New York, Wiley. *83–4*

Hendrick, C. and Costanini, A. (1970) 'Effects of varying trait inconsistency and response requirements on the primacy effect on impression formation', *Journal of Personality and Social Psychology* 15, 158–64. *93*

Henley, M. (1977) *Body Politics: Power, Sex and Non-verbal Communication*, Englewood Cliffs, NJ, Prentice-Hall. *77*

Hermann, M. (1979) 'Indicators of stress in policy makers during foreign policy crises', *Political Psychology* 1, 27–47.

Hodges, B. (1974) 'Effect of volume on relative weighting in impression formation', *Journal of Personality and Social Psychology* 30, 378–81. *93*

Homans, G. (1961) *Social Behavior: Its Elementary Forms*, New York, Harcourt Brace & World. *37, 132*

Hughes, J., Rehm, M. and Rehm, L. (1982) 'Measurement of depression in clinical trials: an overview', *Journal of Clinical Psychiatry* 43 (3), 85–8. *146*

Ickes, W. (1978) 'The enactment of social roles in unstructured dyadic interaction', paper presented at the meeting of the Midwestern Psychological Association, Chicago. *77*

Ickes, W. and Laydon, M. (1978) 'Attributional styles', in J. Harvey, W. Ickes and R. Kidd (eds) *New Directions in Attribution Research*, vol. 2, Hillsdale, NJ, Lawrence Erlbaum. *122*

Izard, C. (1977) *Human Emotions*, New York, Plenum. *III*

Jones, E. and Davis, K. (1965) 'A theory of correspondent inferences: from acts to dispositions', in L. Berkowitz (ed.) *Advances in Experimental Social Psychology*, vol. 2, New York, Academic Press. *85, 94*

Jones, E. and McGillis, P. (1976) 'Correspondent inference and the attribution cube: a comparative reappraisal', in J. Harvey, W. Ickes and R. Kidd (eds) *New Directions in Attribution Research*, vol. I, Hillsdale, NJ, Lawrence Erlbaum. *87*

Jourard, S. (1971) *Self-Disclosure: An Experimental Analysis of the Transparent Self*, New York, Wiley. *125*

Kandel, D. (1978) 'Similarity in real-life adolescent friendship pairs', *Journal of Personality and Social Psychology* 36, 300–12. *135*

Kelley, H. (1967) 'Attribution theory in social psychology', in D. Levine (ed.) *Nebraska Symposium on Motivation*, vol. 15, Lincoln, Nebraska, University of Nebraska Press. *84–6, 114, 132, 139*

Kelly, G. (1955) *A Theory of Personality: The Psychology of Personal Constructs*, 2 vols, New York, Norton. *91*

Kendon, A. (1970) 'Movement coordination in social interaction: some examples described', *Acta Psychologica* 32, 100–25. *74*

Kimble, C. and Forte, R. (1978) 'Simulated and real eye-contact as a function of emotional intensity and message positivity', paper presented at the meeting of the Midwestern Psychological Association. *75*

Kitchens, A. (1974) 'Shape-of-the-table negotiations at the Paris peace talks on Vietnam', in C. Loo (ed.) *Crowding and Behavior*, New York, MFS Information Company. *43*

Knapp, M. (1978) *Non-verbal Communication in Human Interaction*, 2nd edn, New York, Holt, Rinehart & Winston.

Knapp, M., Hart, R. and Dennis, H. (1974) 'An exploration of deception as a communication construct', *Human Communication Research* 1, 15–29. *71*

La France, M. and Carmen, B. (1980) 'The non-verbal display of psychological androgyny', *Journal of Personality and Social Psychology* 38, 36–49. *75*

La France, M. and Mayo, C. (1978) *Moving Bodies: Non-verbal Communication in Social Relationships*, Monterey, California, Brooks/Cole. *72*

Laird, J. (1974) 'Self-attribution of emotion: the effects of expressive behaviour on the quality of emotional experience', *Journal of Personality and Social Psychology* 29, 475–86. *72*

Lakoff, R. (1975) *Language and Woman's Place*, New York, Harper Colophas. *63*

Lalljee, M., Watson, M. and White, P. (1982) 'Explanations, attributions and the social context of unexpected behaviour', *European Journal of Social Psychology* 12 (1), 17–29. *87*

Langer, E. (1975) 'The illusion of control', *Journal of Personality and Social Psychology* 32, 311–28. *102*

Lavrakas, P. and Maier, R. (1979) 'Differences in human ability to judge veracity from the audio medium', *Journal of Research in Personality* 13, 139–53. *72*

Leet-Pellegrini, H. (1980) 'Conversational dominance as a function of gender and expertise', in H. Giles, N. Robinson and P. Smith (eds) *Language: Social Psychological Perspectives*, Oxford, Pergamon Press. *63*

Levinger, G. and Huesmann, L. (1980) 'An incremental exchange perspective on the pair relationship: interpersonal reward and level of involvement', in K. Gergen, M. Greenberg and R. Willis (eds) *Social Exchange: Advances in Theory and Research*, New York, Plenum. *136*

Lewinsohn, D. and Mischel, W. (1980) 'Social competence and depression: the role of illusory self-perception', *Journal of Abnormal Psychology* 89, 203–12. *123*

McArthur, L. (1972) 'The How and What of Why: some determinants and consequences of causal attributions', *Journal of Personality and Social Psychology* 22, 171–93. *85–6*

McArthur, L. and Post, D. (1977) 'Figural emphasis and person perception', *Journal of Experimental Social Psychology* 13, 520–36. *88*

McGuire, W., McGuire, C. and Winton, M. (1979) 'The effects of household sex composition on the salience of one's gender in spontaneous self-concept', *Journal of Experimental Social Psychology* 15, 77–90. *120*

Markus, H. (1977) 'Self-schemata and processing information about the self', *Journal of Personality and Social Psychology* 35, 63–78. *120*

Maslow, A. and Mintz, N. (1956) 'Effects of aesthetic surroundings, I. Initial effect of three aesthetic conditions upon perceiving "energy" and "well-being" in faces', *Journal of Psychology* 41, 247–54. *46*

Meichenbaum, D., Bowers, K. and Ross, R. (1969) 'A behavioural analysis of teachers' expectancy effect', *Journal of Personality and Social Psychology* 13, 306–16. *95*

Milgram, S. (1970) 'The experience of living in cities', *Science* 167, 1461–8. *38, 43*

Miller, L., Murphy, R. and Buss, A. (1981) 'Consciousness of body: private and public', *Journal of Personality and Social Psychology* 41, 397–406. *111*

Modigliani, A. (1968) 'Embarrassment and embarrassibility', *Sociometry* 31, 313–26. *119*

Murstein, B. (1972) 'Physical attractiveness and marital choice', *Journal of Personality and Social Psychology* 22, 8–12. *136*

Nisbett, R. and Ross, L. (1980) *Human Inference: Strategies and Shortcomings*. Englewood Cliffs, NJ, Prentice-Hall. *86, 96, 114, 117, 141, 167*

Nisbett, R. and Wilson, T. (1977a) 'Telling more than we can know: verbal reports on mental processes', *Psychological Review* 84, 231–59. *115*

Nisbett, R. and Wilson, T. (1977b) 'The halo effect: evidence for the unconscious alteration of judgements', *Journal of Personality and Social Psychology* 35, 250–6. *115*

Nisbett, R., Caputo, C., Legant, P. and Marachek, J. (1973) 'Behaviour as seen by the actor and as seen by the observer', *Journal of Personality and Social Psychology* 27, 154–64. *115*

Nogami, G. (1976) 'Crowding: effects of group size, room size or density', *Journal of Applied Social Psychology* 71, 174–208. *44*

Osgood, C., Suci, G. and Tannenbaum, P. (1957) *The Measurement of Meaning*, Urbana, University of Illinois Press. *58*

Phares, E. (1976) *Locus of Control in Personality*, Morristown, NJ, General Learning Press. *108*

Rands, M. and Levinger, G. (1979) 'Implicit theories of relationships: an intergenerational study', *Journal of Personality and Social Psychology* 37, 645–61. *136*

Razran, G. (1950) 'Ethnic dislikes and stereotypes: a laboratory study', *Journal of Abnormal and Social Psychology* 45, 7–27. *83*

Rogers, C. (1957) 'The necessary and sufficient conditions of therapeutic personality change', *Journal of Consultant Psychology* 22, 95–103. *4*

Rogers, C. (1961) *On Becoming a Person*, Boston, Mass., Houghton Mifflin. *125, 141*

Romney, A., Shephard, R. and Nerlove, S. (1972) *Multi-dimensional Scaling: Theory and Applications in the Behavioral Sciences*, vol. 2, New York, Seminar Press. *58*

Rosenberg, M. (1965) *Society and the Adolescent Self-Image*, Princeton, NJ, Princeton University Press. *122*

Rosenberg, S. and Jones, R. (1972) 'A method for investigating and representing an implicit theory of personality: Theodore Dreiser's view of people', *Journal of Personality and Social Psychology* 20, 372–86. *90*

Rosenberg, S. and Sedlak, A. (1972) 'Structural representations of implicit personality theory', in L. Berkowitz (ed.) *Advances in Experimental Social Psychology*, vol. 6, New York, Academic Press. *30*

Ross, L., Amabile, T. and Steinmetz, J. (1977) 'Social roles, social control and biases in social perception processes', *Journal of Personality and Social Psychology* 35, 485–94. *88*

Rotter, J. (1966) 'Generalized expectancies for internal versus external control of reinforcement', *Psychological Monographs* 80, 609. *107–8*

Rumelhart, D. (1975) 'Notes on a schema for stories', in D. Bobrow and A. Collins (eds) *Representation and Understanding: Studies in Cognitive Science*, New York, Academic Press. *54*

Schachter, S. (1964) 'The interaction of cognitive and physiological determinants of emotional state', in L. Berkowitz (ed.) *Advances in Experimental Social Psychology*, vol. I, New York, Academic Press. *III*

Schachter, S. and Singer, J. (1962) 'Cognitive, social, and physiological determinants of emotional states', *Psychological Review* 69, 379–99. *112–13*

Scheflen, A. (1964) 'The significance of posture in communication systems', *Psychiatry* 27, 316–21. *74, 76*

Schegloff, E. and Sacks, H. (1973) 'Opening-up closings', *Semiotica* 8, 289–327. *10–11, 156*

Schultz, R. (1976) 'Effects of control and predictability on the psychological well-being of the institutionalized aged', *Journal of Personality and Social Psychology* 33, 563–73. *104*

Schwarz, C. (1957) 'Problems for psychiatric nurses in playing a new role on a mental hospital ward', in M. Greenblatt, D. Levinson and R. Williams (eds) *The Patient and the Mental Hospital*, New York, Free Press, 402–26. *24*

Schwarz, S. (1970) 'Elicitation of moral obligation and self-sacrificing behaviour: an experimental study of volunteering to be a bone-marrow donor', *Journal of Personality and Social Psychology* 15, 283–93. *106*

Seeman, M. and Evans, J. (1962) 'Alienation and learning in a hospital setting', *American Sociological Review* 27, 772–83. *108*

Seligman, M. (1975) *Helplessness: On Depression, Development and Death*, San Francisco, W.H. Freeman. *103*

Shanteau, J. and Nagy, G. (1979) 'Probability of acceptance in dating choice', *Journal of Personality and Social Psychology* 37, 522–33. *136*

Skinner, B. F. (1953) *Science and Human Behavior*, New York, Macmillan. *129, 138–9*

Slobin, D., Miller, S. and Parker, L. (1968) 'Forms of address and social relations in a business organization', *Journal of Personality and Social Psychology* 8, 289–93. *125*

Snyder, M. (1974) 'Self-monitoring of expressive behaviour', *Journal of Personality and Social Psychology* 36, 526–37. *119*

Snyder, M., Tanke, E. and Berscheid, E. (1977) 'Social perception and interpersonal behaviour: on the self-fulfilling nature of social stereotypes', *Journal of Personality and Social Psychology* 35, 656–66. *94, 118*

Solomon, S. and Saxe, L. (1977) 'What is intelligent as well as attractive is good', *Personality and Social Psychology Bulletin* 3, 670–3. *136*

Sommer, R. (1969) *Personal Space: The Behavioral Basis of Design*, Englewood Cliffs, NJ, Prentice-Hall. *42*

Suls, J. and Gastorf, J. (1977) *Social Comparison Processes*, Washington DC, Hemisphere/Halsted.

Swann, J. and Read, S. (1981) 'Self-verification processes: how we sustain our self-conceptions', *Journal of Experimental Social Psychology* 17, 351–72. *121, 124*

Swenson, C. (1978) 'Love, problems, and the development of the marriage relationship', unpublished manuscript, Purdue University. *137*

Taylor, S., Fiske, S., Close, M., Anderson, C. and Ruderman, A. (1979) 'Solo status as a psychological variable: the power of being distinctive', unpublished manuscript, Harvard University. *87*

Thibault, J. and Kelley, H. (1978) *Interpersonal Relations: a Theory of Interdependence*, New York, Wiley. *132, 134–5, 137*

Thomas, W. and Thomas, D. (1928) *The Child in America*, New York, Knopf. *27*

Trower, P., Bryant, B. and Argyle, M. (1978) *Social Skills and Mental Health*, London, Methuen. *142, 156, 163–4, 167*

Wallwork, J. (1969) *Language and Linguistics*, London, Heinemann Educational. *57*

Walster, E. and Festinger, L. (1962) 'The effectiveness of "overhead" persuasive communications', *Journal of Abnormal and Social Psychology* 65, 395–402. *105*

Walster, E., Walster, G. and Berscheid, E. (1978) *Equity Theory and Research*, Newton, Mass., Allyn & Bacon. *137*

Watson, O. and Graves, T. (1966) 'Quantitative research in proxemic behavior', *American Anthropologist* 68, 971–85. *76*

Weinberg, M. (1965) 'Sexual modesty and the nudist camp', *Social Problems* XII (3), 315.

Weiss, J. and Brown, P. (1977) 'Self-insight error in the explanation of mood', unpublished manuscript, Harvard University. *116*

Whitcher, S. and Fisher, J. (1979) 'Multi-dimensional reactions to therapeutic touch in a hospital setting', *Journal of Personality and Social Psychology* 37, 87–96. *77*

Wicklund, R. (1975) 'Objective self-awareness', in L. Berkowitz (ed.) *Advances in Experimental Social Psychology*, vol. 8, New York, Academic Press. *101*

Wicklund, R. and Brehm, J. (1967) 'Effect of censorship on attitude change and desire to hear a communication', unpublished manuscript, Duke University. *105*

Wools, R. and Canter, D. (1970) 'The effect of the meaning of buildings on behaviour', *Applied Ergonomics* I (3), 144–50. *45*

Worchel, S. and Brehm, J. (1971) 'Direct and implied social restoration of freedom', *Journal of Personality and Social Psychology* 18, 294–304. *106*

Wortman, C. and Brehm, J. (1975) 'Responses to uncontrollable outcomes: an interpretation of reactance theory and the learned helplessness model', in L. Berkowitz (ed.) *Advances in Experimental Social Psychology*, vol. 8, New York, Academic Press. *103, 106*

Subject index

The references section of this book serves as a name index. Names are included in this index only where there is no corresponding literature citation; in most cases these are the names of historical personages.

179